Solutions Development

*An Authorized
Teradata Certified
Professional Program
Study Guide*

Exam TE0-145

First Edition

ISBN 978-0-9894005-4-1
Printed by Cerulium Corporation

**Stephen Wilmes
Mark Ferguson**

Copyright

© Copyright 2014 by Cerulium Corporation. All rights reserved. No part of this publication may be reproduced, stored in a retrieval system, or transmitted in any form or by any means, electronic, mechanical, scanning or otherwise, except as permitted by Sections 107 and 108 of the 1976 United States Copyright Act without prior permission of the copyright owner.

Limit of liability/disclaimer of warranty: The publisher and authors make no representation or warranties with respect to the accuracy and completeness of the contents of this work and specifically disclaim all warranties, including without limitation warranties of fitness for a particular purpose. Neither the publisher nor the authors shall be liable for damages arising from the use of information contained herein.

Trademarks

The following names are registered names and/or trademarks, and are used throughout the book: Teradata, Teradata BYNET, Teradata Administrator, Teradata SQL Assistant, Teradata Raising Intelligence, Teradata Decision Experts, Teradata Source Experts, Raising Intelligence, Smarter.Faster.Wins., Active Enterprise Intelligence, DECISIONCAST, WEBANALYST, MYCOMMERCE, SEECHAIN, SEERISK, CLARAVIEW, GRIDSCALE, and XKOTO are registered trademarks and/or products of Teradata Corporation. Microsoft Windows and .NET are either registered trademarks or trademarks of Microsoft Corporation. Sun Java and GoldenGate is a trademark or registered trademark of Oracle Corporation in the U.S. or other countries. In addition to these product names, all brand and product names in this manual are trademarks of their respective holders in the United States and/or other countries.

Special Acknowledgement

A special thank you to the following individuals that contributed to the Study Guide content: Barbara Christjohn, Kaylee Parker, and David Micheletto.

About the Author - Steve Wilmes

Steve Wilmes founded Cerulium Corporation in 2007. As Chief Executive Officer, his goal is to establish Cerulium as a premier data warehousing Technology Company. Cerulium's strategic growth is globally focused on six lines of business including education, consulting, BI solutions, productivity tools, application integration and assessment services. These lines of business have been highly successful by utilizing strategic data warehousing solutions provided by Teradata that spans across the consumer, and commercial markets.

Mr. Wilmes has over 20 years of experience in the computer industry and is known to be a detail oriented, results-focused leader. He is an internationally recognized expert in several aspects of data warehousing including hardware, software, SQL, operating systems, implementation, data integration, database administration, and BI solutions.

Mr. Wilmes earned a bachelor's degree in business administration and economics in 1994 from Augsburg College and he is also a Teradata Certified Master.

Mr. Wilmes resides just outside of Columbia, South Carolina, with his wife, Becky. He has been involved with numerous civic, educational, and business organizations throughout his career. Some of his more recent associations include working with the Richland County Sheriff's Department – Region 4 Community Member, and volunteer for local organizations where he shares his technical expertise.

About the Author - Mark Ferguson

Mark Ferguson is a Vice President of Cerulium Corporation. In addition to Consulting on a daily basis, Mr. Ferguson is also responsible for Marketing and Corporate Branding for Cerulium. His experience spans the healthcare, telecommunications, pharmaceutical, retail, and publishing industries at several Fortune 500 companies and the U.S. Government. He has worked with, designed, and managed some of the biggest data warehouses in the world. While specializing in providing customized Teradata solutions, he has also worked on many complex Business Intelligence, Analytics, and Big Data projects.

Mr. Ferguson has been in the Data Warehousing industry for over 15 years. While the overwhelming bulk of his career has been working directly with Teradata, he has also worked with many other RDBMS and Big Data platforms as well as many different Business Intelligence software vendors. He shares his passion for data quality and integrity with teams he manages, resulting in impeccable solutions.

Mr. Ferguson resides near Nashville, TN with his wife, Kelly, and their two children. He is enthusiastically involved in youth sports and volunteers for many civic and philanthropic activities. He has utilized his expertise in photography to help charitable organizations such as the Susan G. Komen foundation and Habitat for Humanity.

Table of Contents

Chapter 1: The Teradata Certified Professional Program 1
    Pursue Teradata Certification with Confidence™ 1
    Your Teradata 14 Certification Upgrade Roadmap 3
    Certification... Knowledge Building to Mastery 6
    Path to Teradata 14 Mastery 7
    Exam Registration 7
    Where to Find More Information 8

Chapter 2 – Data Modeling 9
    Certification Objectives 9
    Before You Begin 9
    Logical Data Modeling 9
    Access Layer Modeling (Semantic Data Modeling) 12
    Physical Data Modeling 16
    Chapter 2: Practice Questions 20

Chapter 3 – Space Usage and Table Types 23
    Certification Objectives 23
    Before You Begin 23
    Perm/Spool/Temp Space 23
    Permanent Space Terminology 24
    CREATE TABLE Definitions 26
    SET/MULTISET Tables 28
    Derived Temporary Tables 29
    Volatile Temporary Tables 31
    Global Temporary Tables 35
    Queue Tables 37
    Chapter 3: Practice Questions 41

Chapter 4 – SQL Optimization Strategies 45
    Certification Objectives 45
    Before You Begin 45
    Locking 46
    Recursive Queries 51
    Views 54
    Macros 56
    Stored Procedures 59

Ordered Analytic Functions 63
Date/Time Manipulation 65
Period Data Types 71
Period Manipulation 72
Calendar Functions 74
Business Calendars 75
Nulls 76
Row vs. Set Manipulation 80
Collect Statistics 83
Chapter 4: Practice Questions 94
Chapter 5 - Indexes 97
Certification Objectives 97
Before You Begin 97
PI/SI Access Chart 98
NUSI Bitmapping 99
Value-Ordered NUSI 101
Hash NUSI 102
PPI – Partitioned Primary Index 106
MLPPI 110
No Primary Index (NoPI) tables 124
Column-Partitioned Tables 125
Column Partitioning and Query Performance 125
Horizontal Partitioning 125
Vertical Partitioning 126
Join Indexes 127
Sparse Indexes 138
Chapter 5: Practice Questions 147
Chapter 6 – Joins and Explain 151
Certification Objectives 151
Before You Begin 151
Joins 151
Join Strategies 153
Join Types 154
Inner Joins 154
Outer Joins 154

    Join Strategies 156
    Merge Joins 156
    Nested Joins 159
    Hash Joins 160
    Inclusion and Exclusion Join 160
    Product Joins 160
    EXPLAIN Terminology 161
    Chapter 6: Practice Questions 174
Chapter 7 – Utilities 177
    Certification Objectives 177
    Before You Begin 177
    BTEQ 178
    FastLoad 181
    FastExport 185
    MultiLoad 188
    TPump 192
    Teradata Parallel Transporter 194
    Utility Limits 202
    Parameters 205
    CLOBs and BLOBs 211
    Client performance considerations 212
    SET vs. MULTISET table loading 220
    Duplicate Row Elimination 220
    Data availability and integrity 221
    Load Strategies 224
    Chapter 7: Practice Questions 226
Chapter 8 – Data Integration and Performance 231
    Certification Objectives 231
    Development Choices 232
    Normalization 233
    Event driven 235
    Business Intelligence (BI) 236
    Active Data Warehouse 238
    Data integration 241
    Data access 242

- Unicode 243
- Considerations for Loading PPI and MLPPI Tables 244
- Considerations for Loading NoPI Tables 245
- Chapter 8: Practice Questions 246

Chapter 9 – Maintaining Data Integrity 249
- Certification Objectives 249
- Before You Begin 249
- Triggers 250
- RI Constraints 253
- Check Constraints 257
- Transaction mode 258
- Multi-statement requests 263
- Multi-request Transactions 264
- User Defined Functions (UDFs) 268
- Chapter 9: Practice Questions 271

Chapter 10 – Performance Monitoring Tools & Facilities 275
- Certification Objectives 275
- Before You Begin 275
- Access Logging 275
- Database Query Log (DBQL) 277
- Teradata Query Scheduler 278
- Teradata Active System Management (TASM) 279
- Teradata Viewpoint 280
- Teradata Workload Analyzer 281
- Priority Scheduler 282
- Workload Designer 286
- Workload Health 286
- Resource Partitions and Performance Groups 287
- Schmon Utility 293
- Teradata Analyst Pack 293
- Visual Explain 294
- Statistics Wizard 295
- Index Wizard 297
- Teradata System Emulation Tool (TSET) 302
- ResUsage 309

    Locking Logger 324
    DBC.AMPUsage 326
    Chapter 10: Practice Questions 328
Chapter 11 – Solution Planning 333
    Certification Objectives 333
    Before You Begin 333
    Capacity planning 334
    Security planning 336
    Migration Planning 340
    Administration planning 341
    Data integration 341
    Dual system architecture 348
    Chapter 11: Practice Questions 353
APPENDIX A – Review Question Answers 357
INDEX 359

Chapter 1: The Teradata Certified Professional Program

Pursue Teradata Certification with Confidence™

The Teradata Certified Professional Program (TCPP), launched in 1999, develops and manages Teradata's premier, and only, certification testing program. Teradata authorized training and proctored exams, available globally to customers, partners, associates, and students, are instrumental in establishing an industry-standard measure of technical competence for IT professionals using Teradata technology. Recognized as a leader in Data Warehouse RDBMS technology and valued by major global companies using Teradata, more than 57,000 Teradata Certifications have been awarded.

The new Teradata 14 Certification Track consists of seven exams that combine for achievement of six certifications and provides a logical progression for specific job roles. Starting with the core Teradata 14 Certified Professional credential, individuals have an opportunity to demonstrate knowledge by achieving Certification as a Technical Specialist, Database Administrator, Solutions Developer, Enterprise Architect, and the most prestigious Teradata Certification – Teradata 14 Certified Master.

The purpose of this Certification Exam Study Guide is to assist you with your goal to become Teradata Certified. This Guide will provide focused content areas, high level explanations around the key areas of focus, and help you to determine areas of further study prior to sitting for the Teradata Certification examination.

Although the Exam Study Guide will assist you in exam preparation, you must be knowledgeable of the subject areas in order to pass the exam. This Guide is intended for individuals who have completed the recommended training and have the recommended amount of

Teradata 14 Solutions Development

Teradata experience. **We do not guarantee that you will pass the exam simply by reading the Exam Study Guide.** Only hard work, hands-on experience, and a positive attitude will help you to achieve exam success. We wish you the very best of luck!

> *"When hiring, I always look for Teradata Certified Professionals. Not only does it provide me a good understanding of a candidate's knowledge level, it also shows a commitment to continuous learning and self-improvement. That's a great trait to have in every employee and the Teradata Certified Professional Program makes it easy to recognize."*
>
> *Teradata Certified Master, Insurance Industry*

The flowchart and matrix below are designed to help you define a path to the knowledge, skills, and experience needed to achieve Teradata 14 Certifications.

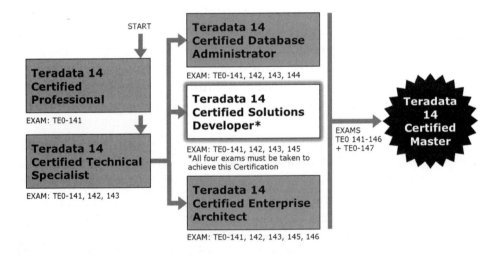

Your Teradata 14 Certification Upgrade Roadmap

Teradata 12 Certified candidates, in good standing, are eligible to take the *Teradata 14 Bridge from Teradata 12 Exam (TE0-14B)*. The Bridge exam is a hybrid of all three (3) Teradata baseline Certification exams, and covers content changes to Teradata Basics, Teradata SQL and Teradata Physical Design & Implementation exams.

A passed exam result on the Bridge exam will yield the *Teradata 14 Certified Technical Specialist* designation. A candidate may then continue on the Teradata 14 track until achieving the desired Certification level.

Teradata 14 Certifications

Teradata 14 Certified Professional

Exams Required:
- TE0-141 – Teradata 14 Basics

Must be passed before continuing on certification path

Recommended Teradata Experience:
6-12 months

Recommended Preparation Courses:
- Introduction to the Teradata Database

Teradata 14 Certified Technical Specialist

Exams Required:
- TE0-141 – Teradata 14 Basics
- TE0-142 – Teradata 14 SQL
- TE0-143 – Teradata 14 Physical Design and Implementation

3 Exams to be passed in sequential order

Recommended Teradata Experience:
1-2 years

Recommended Preparation Courses:
- Introduction to the Teradata Database
- Teradata SQL
- Advanced Teradata SQL
- Physical Database Design
- Physical Database Tuning

Teradata 14 Solutions Development

Teradata 14 Certified Database Administrator

Exams Required:
- TE0-141 – Teradata 14 Basics
- TE0-142 – Teradata 14 SQL
- TE0-143 – Teradata 14 Physical Design and Implementation
- TE0-144 – Teradata 14 Database Administration

4 Exams to be passed in sequential order

Recommended Teradata Experience:
2-3 years

Recommended Preparation Courses:
- Introduction to the Teradata Database
- Teradata SQL
- Advanced Teradata SQL
- Physical Database Design
- Physical Database Tuning
- Teradata Application Utilities
- Teradata Parallel Transporter
- Teradata Warehouse Management
- Teradata Warehouse Administration

Teradata 14 Certified Solutions Developer

Exams Required:
- TE0-141 – Teradata 14 Basics
- TE0-142 – Teradata 14 SQL
- TE0-143 – Teradata 14 Physical Design and Implementation
- TE0-145 – Teradata 14 Solutions Development

4 Exams to be passed in sequential order

Recommended Teradata Experience:
2-3 years

Recommended Preparation Courses:
- Introduction to the Teradata Database
- Teradata SQL
- Advanced Teradata SQL
- Physical Database Design
- Physical Database Tuning
- Teradata Application Utilities
- Teradata Parallel Transporter
- Teradata Application Design and Development

THE TERADATA CERTIFIED PROFESSIONAL PROGRAM

Teradata 14 Certified Enterprise Architect

Exams Required:
- TE0-141 – Teradata 14 Basics
- TE0-142 – Teradata 14 SQL
- TE0-143 – Teradata 14 Physical Design and Implementation
- TE0-145 – Teradata 14 Solutions Development
- TE0-146 – Teradata 14 Enterprise Architecture

5 Exams to be passed in sequential order

Recommended Teradata Experience:
2-3 years

Recommended Preparation Courses:

- Introduction to the Teradata Database
- Teradata SQL
- Advanced Teradata SQL
- Physical Database Design
- Physical Database Tuning
- Teradata Application Utilities
- Teradata Parallel Transporter
- Teradata Warehouse Management
- Teradata Warehouse Administration
- Teradata Application Design and Development

Teradata 14 Certified Master*

Exams Required:
- TE0-141 - TE0-146: Successful completion of all exams **PLUS:**
- TE0-147 – Teradata 14 Comprehensive Mastery Exam

7 Exams to be passed in sequential order

*Path for Teradata 12 Certified Masters
- TE0-147 – Teradata 14 Comprehensive Mastery Exam

Recommended Teradata Experience:
A minimum 5 years practical hands-on experience is highly recommended

Recommended Preparation Courses:
- Introduction to the Teradata Database
- Teradata SQL
- Advanced Teradata SQL
- Physical Database Design
- Physical Database Tuning
- Teradata Application Utilities
- Teradata Parallel Transporter
- Teradata Warehouse Management
- Teradata Warehouse Administration
- Teradata Application Design and Development

Teradata 14 Solutions Development

Note: Formal education recommendations may vary based on previous training and relevant job experience.

Certification... Knowledge Building to Mastery

Competition is fierce. Differentiate yourself while building critical IT technology knowledge and skills. Trust Teradata Certification to help you build the expertise employers are looking for in a demanding, data-driven global business environment. Teradata developed a new generation of certification exams that bring premium value to Teradata 14 Certification credentials.

Top 10 "What's new about the Teradata 14 Certification Track?"
1. Seven exams with all new content based upon the following database releases: Teradata Database 13.0, Teradata Database 13.1, Teradata Database 14.0 (including SLES 11)
2. The *"Teradata 14 Bridge from Teradata 12"* Exam allows Teradata 12 certified candidates to move, or "bridge", from the Teradata 12 Certification track to the Teradata 14 Certification track without starting the track from the beginning.
3. Eligibility-based exams to ensure compliance with Teradata Certification requirements (Bridge and Masters exams only)
4. Teradata 12 Certified Masters will take just one exam to update to Teradata 14 Certified Master status.
5. A Qualification exam is not required for those that have achieved a Teradata 12 Master Certification.
6. A new Candidate Agreement and revised security measures are in place to protect the value of your investment and integrity of all exams and certifications.
7. Newly designed electronic certificates, wallet cards, and logos.
8. An easy Certification verification process for individuals and employers.
9. More rigorous certification criteria including a combination of training, study, and practical, hands-on experience.

10. A team of dedicated, experienced, and knowledgeable individuals with a passion to help you achieve your Teradata Certification goals!

Path to Teradata 14 Mastery

A Teradata Certified Master enjoys a distinct advantage in the global marketplace. Employers seek Teradata Certified staff with verifiable knowledge and skills that support their business-critical Teradata systems. The TCPP process helps those individuals who want to deepen their knowledge and build their skills to the highest level.

The path to achieve Teradata 14 Certified Master status is summarized in the matrix below.

If You Are...	Exams Required for Teradata 14 Master Certification
Starting on the Teradata 14 Certification Track	• TE0-141 – TE0-147 All 7 Exams required
Teradata 12 Certified Master	TE0-147: Teradata 14 Comprehensive Mastery Exam

Exam Registration

All Teradata Certification exams are administered and proctored by authorized Prometric Testing Centers. Schedule exams at any authorized Prometric Testing Center by phone or online. In the US and Canada, you may call 1-877-887-6868. A listing of Prometric telephone numbers, by country, is available at:

www.prometric.com/Teradata. Some countries do not offer online registration.

Where to Find More Information

Teradata Corporation's official certification exams and credentials are developed, copyrighted, and managed solely by the Teradata Certified Professional Program (TCPP) team. There are no other Teradata authorized exams, certifications, or legitimate credentials in the IT industry. To achieve your training and certification goals, pursue only authorized processes and approved courses of study as outlined on the official TCPP Website: www.Teradata.com/Certification. A mobile app with access to all study guides, practice questions, and many more Teradata Certification and related resources is also available for a variety of devices. Please refer to the web site for additional information.

Chapter 2 – Data Modeling

Certification Objectives

- ✓ Identify the characteristics of the logical data model.
- ✓ Identify the characteristics of the semantic data model.
- ✓ Identify the characteristics of the physical data model.

Before You Begin

You should be familiar with the following terms and concepts.

Terms	Key Concepts
Primary Key	Unique identifier of a row
Foreign Key	Identifies a relationship
Logical Modeling	Identify Entities, Relations, and Attributes
Normalization	The process of placing non-key attributes into their proper relation.
Physical Modeling	Using the information gathered in the Activity Transaction Model (ATM) process

Logical Data Modeling

The requirements analysis phase of the design process reveals the real world objects and their attributes that the database must represent as well as the relationships among them.

The logical database design phase formalizes the objects, or entities, and their relationships. It ensures that the modeled entities are modified by attributes that uniquely pertain to them. No attribute should appear in an entity unless it describes the uniqueness identifier for the entity -- its primary key.

Teradata 14 Solutions Development

There are a few things you should consider when designing your Teradata Data Warehouse, but none of them involve taking any nontraditional approaches to the task:

One major consideration is whether third party vendors are Teradata partners. Query tools, for example, should take advantage of Teradata optimizations (i.e. Online Analytical Processing).

Another major consideration is that if you intend to perform a mix of ad hoc tactical and decision support queries or if you plan to undertake any serious data mining projects, then you should limit the physical denormalization of the database to a minimum.

For example, if you perform frequent ROLAP analyses of your data and performance is not what you expect to see – after exploring all database performance options - consider off-loading the data to a dependent data mart designed around the multidimensional model that many OLAP proponents advocate. You should not denormalize the entire database just to support a few OLAP applications.

If you plan to use data mining technology, then a normalized database is the key to your success. Data mining techniques do not perform well in a denormalized environment.

The two principal commercial uses for relational systems are Online Transaction Processing (OLTP) and Decision Support (DSS). The access patterns of these two approaches are very different and they make very different demands on the underlying database engine.

The following chart compares the two processing forms:

OLTP Transaction	Attribute	DSS Query
No	Multiple tables scanned	Yes
No	Large volumes of data examined	Yes
No	Processing intensive	Yes

DATA MODELING

OLTP Transaction	Attribute	DSS Query
No	Response time is a function of database size	Yes

Figure 2.1

Any design process must begin with the knowledge of what is to be designed. This includes not only the proposed morphology of the end product but also the systems, policies, and procedures - the processes - of the designed product.

This fundamental knowledge is derived through a process of accumulating facts about how the eventual users use the product. The process includes, at minimum, the following tasks:

- Interviewing notable employees, both management and support staff, for information such as the following:
    - What information do they need?
    - What is the source of that information?
    - What are the tasks involved with creating and reporting the information?
    - How is the information used?
- Gathering all input screens and reports generated by the legacy system and interviewing management and support staff about what is right and wrong about these components as well as determining what type of new or different input and report items should be added to the new system.
- Compiling and circulating the cumulative research information you have gathered to obtain affirmation of its accuracy from all involved parties.
- Writing a requirements specification from the approved research information and making it available to the designer of the logical database.

Access Layer Modeling (Semantic Data Modeling)

Semantic data modeling consists of identifying Entities, documenting their relationship to one another, and populating them with attributes.

ENTITIES

An entity is a database object that represents a thing in the real world. Entities are expressed as nouns. All entities are nouns, but not all nouns are entities. Some nouns are attributes of entities or relations.

Entities can be concrete, like buildings and employees or they can be more abstract things like departments and accounts.

Entities fall into one of four categories, as shown in Figure 2.2:

Entity Type	Definition	Example
Major	An entity with relatively large cardinality and degree that is updated frequently.	Order table
Minor	An entity with small cardinality and degree that is rarely updated. Minor entities are typically used in a single, 1:M association, and their primary key is often nonnumeric.	Nation Code table
Supertype	A generic entity that is a superclass of one or more subtype entities. Supertype and subtype entities model the same real world entity at a high level.	Publications table

DATA MODELING

Entity Type	Definition	Example
	Supertypes must, by definition, have one or more reciprocal subtypes.	
Subtype	A specific entity that is a disjoint subclass of one and only one supertype entity. Subtype and supertype entities model the same real world entity at a high level. Subtype entities typically have a higher degree than their supertypes, with the additional attributes describing detailed characteristics of the subtype that distinguish it from the other subtype entities of a mutual supertype.	Book table Magazine table Professional Journal table Conference Proceedings table (all as subtypes of the supertype Publications)

Figure 2.2

Entities are described by a single-column, non-decomposable attribute.

RELATIONSHIPS

A relationship is an association among two or more entities or other relationships. Relationships are expressed as verbs. Relationships among entities are described by one of three ratios:

- One-to-One (1:1)
- One-to Many (1:M)
- Many-to-Many (M:M)

Relationships are defined through Primary Keys and Foreign Keys.

ATTRIBUTES

An attribute is a characteristic of an entity. Every entity has at least one attribute--its primary key. Attributes are expressed as nouns qualified by adjectives that clarify their role. An attribute plays one of three possible roles in any table:

- Primary key attributes identify the entity or relationship modeled by a table.
- Primary key attributes are said to be *identifier* attributes because they uniquely identify an instance of an entity.
- Foreign key attributes define relationships between and among entities or among entities and relationships.

A foreign key attribute can be an identifier attribute if it is part of a composite primary key; otherwise, foreign key attributes are descriptor attributes.

Non-key attributes further describe the entity or relationship modeled by a table. Non-key attributes are said to be *descriptor* attributes because they specify a non-unique characteristic of an instance of an entity.

DERIVATIVE ATTRIBUTES

So-called derivative attributes violate the rules of normalization in relational theory because they are not atomic. A derivative attribute is any attribute that can be derived by calculation from other data in the model.

The issue of derivative attributes should not concern you during the logical design phase other than knowing that they should not be modeled. Derivative attributes are an important consideration for physical database design, where they are often modeled as a means for enhancing system performance.

DATA MODELING

Note that the Teradata Database offers several features like hash and join indexes, aggregate join indexes, and global temporary tables that reduce the temptation to denormalize the physical design of your base tables by using derivative attributes.

NORMALIZATION

In the design of a relational database management system (RDBMS), the process of organizing data to minimize redundancy is called normalization. The goal of database normalization is to decompose relationships with anomalies in order to produce smaller, well-structured relations.

Normalization usually involves dividing large tables into smaller (and less redundant) tables and defining relationships between them. The objective is to isolate data so that additions, deletions, and modifications of a field can be made in just one table and then propagated throughout the rest of the database via the defined relationships. The intent of normalizing a relational database can be reduced to one simple aphorism: **One Fact in One Place.**

Note: Every non-key attribute must describe *the key, the whole key, and nothing but the key*.

First Normal Form (1NF)

This means that a field can contain one value and one value only. No hierarchies of data values are allowed. This concept is sometimes referred to as the elimination of repeating groups from a relation.

Second Normal Form (2NF)

A relation in 1NF is also in 2NF if any one of the following statements is also true:

- The primary key is not composite.
- There are no non-key attributes in the relation.
- Every non-key attribute is dependent on the complete set of primary key attributes.

The first two bullets in this list are trivial cases. It is the third bullet that provides a truly generalized definition for 2NF.

Third Normal Form (3NF)

A relation is said to be in Third Normal Form when it is in Second Normal Form and both of the following are true:

- Every non-key attribute depends on all attributes of the primary key: the *entire* primary key.
- No non-key attribute is functionally dependent on another non-key attribute of the relation.

Physical Data Modeling

Once the data model has been defined, the next step is to do Activity Transaction Modeling (ATM) against the model. The goals of the ATM process are as follows:

- Define all domains and constraints.
- Identify all applications.
- Model application processing activities including their transactions and run frequencies.
- Model each transaction using the following information:
    - Identify tables used.
    - Identify columns required for value and join access.
    - Estimate qualifying cardinalities.
    - Summarize value and join access information across all transactions.

- Add data demographics to the Table Access Summary by Columns report.
- Analyze Table cardinalities
- Review column value distributions
- Determine column change ratings

Armed with that information, the relations in the logical model become tables in the physical model.

The physical model defines the Primary Index for each table, along with any Secondary Indexes, Referential Integrity constraints, and data integrity constraints.

The following list of factors illustrates how complex the selection of Teradata Database indexes is, and how important the information gleaned by following the ATM processes is:

- Nonspecific Factors
    - Degree of normalization of the database
    - How the Optimizer might use the index
    - Table type indexed
    - Major entity
    - Minor entity
    - Sub-entity
    - Relationship
- Primary index partitioning type
    - Non-partitioned
    - Partitioned
    - Single-level
    - Multilevel

- Space utilization factors
  - How much space does the index occupy?
  - Type of data protection specified
- Demographic factors
  - Cardinality of the table
  - Number of distinct column values
  - Maximum rows per value
  - Columns most frequently used to access table rows
  - Are rows most commonly accessed by values or by a join?
  - Degree of skew of column values
- Application factors
  - In which application environment are rows most commonly accessed?
  - Decision support
  - OLTP
  - Event queues
  - Tactical queries
  - Ad hoc queries
  - Range queries
  - Batch reporting
  - Batch maintenance
- Transaction factors
  - How are transactions written?
  - How are transactions parceled?
  - What levels and types of locking does a transaction require?
  - How long does the transaction hold locks?
- DML Factors
  - Number of DELETE operations and when they occur
  - Number of INSERT operations and when they occur
  - Number of UPDATE operations and when they occur

The Physical model may also include denormalization descriptors such as:

- Views
- Join Indexes
- Aggregate Join Indexes
- Global Temporary tables
- Dimensional modeling tables

Chapter 2: Practice Questions

1. Which Normal Form eliminates repeating groups?
    a. First Normal Form
    b. Second Normal Form
    c. Third Normal Form

2. Which of the following should never be included in the model?
    a. Candidate keys
    b. Derivative attributes
    c. M:M:M relations
    d. Recursive relations

3. Which phrase describes Third Normal Form (3NF)?
    a. Every non-key attribute is dependent on the complete set of primary key attributes.
    b. No non-key attribute is functionally dependent on another non-key attribute of the relation.
    c. The primary key is not composite.

4. Which phrase best describes the goal of normalization?
    a. The key, the whole key, and nothing but the key.
    b. One fact in one place.
    c. Tuning for OLTP transactions.

5. Supertype and Subtype are examples of:
    a. Attributes
    b. Relations
    c. Entities

Chapter Notes

Utilize this space for notes, key points to remember, diagrams, areas of further study, etc.

Chapter 3 - Space Usage and Table Types

Certification Objectives

✓ Given a scenario, identify which kind of table should be used.

Before You Begin

You should be familiar with the following terms and concepts.

Terms	Key Concepts
Disk space	What are the three types, and what consumes the space.
Duplicate rows	Where they are allowed.
Data persistence	How long does data last in various table types.
Table definitions	How to declare various table types.
Queue Tables	How to set them up and utilize them.

Perm/Spool/Temp Space

PERM SPACE

Perm space is allocated at the database/user level, not at the individual table level. It represents the total number of bytes (including table headers) currently allocated for data tables, indexes, stored procedures, triggers, and permanent journals residing in a particular database/user.

The allocated space is divided equally among all of the AMPs. If any AMP utilizes its allocated amount, the database is considered "full", and an error message is returned to the requestor.

Permanent Space Terminology

CurrentPerm

The total number of bytes (including table headers) currently allocated to existing data tables, indexes, stored procedures, triggers, and permanent journals residing in a particular database/user.

PeakPerm

The largest number of bytes ever used to store data in a user or database since the last reset of this value to zero.

Note: These values are maintained on each AMP. To reset the PeakPerm value to zero, use the DBC.ClearPeakDisk macro.

MaxPerm

The maximum number of bytes available for storage of all (current and future) data tables, indexes, stored procedures, triggers, and permanent journals owned by a particular database/user, as shown in the following diagram.

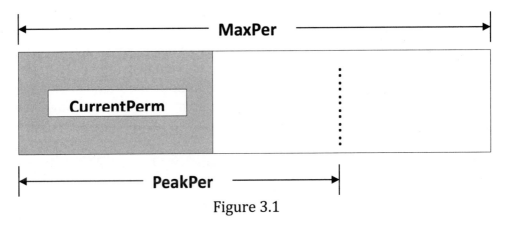

Figure 3.1

SPACE USAGE AND TABLE TYPES

SPOOL SPACE

Spool space is work space used by the system in processing SQL requests. Only users consume spool space, databases do not. The spool limit assigned to a user cannot exceed the spool limit of the immediate parent. The spool limit is divided evenly across all of the AMPs, and represents a threshold that no AMP can exceed.

The DBA specifies the spool limit of each user, taking into consideration the tables they access to reduce the impact of "runaway" transactions, such as accidental Cartesian product joins.

TEMP SPACE

Temp space specifies the limit of space available for global temporary tables. This limit is divided equally among all of the AMPs.

The value may not exceed the limit of:

- The creator or modifier of the profile, when setting TEMPORARY in a profile.
- The immediate owner of the user being created or modified, if a profile does not apply.

CREATE TABLE Definitions

Figure 3.2 shows the general syntax of the CREATE TABLE.

```
CREATE [SET/MULTISET]  [VOLATILE/GLOBAL TEMPORARY]
TABLE tablename
      <Create Table Options>
      <Column Definitions>
      <Table-level Constraints>
      <Index Definitions>;
```
Figure 3.2

The following table expands on these options.

Create Table options	Specify physical attributes of table:
	    Fallback
	    Journaling
	    Freespace
	    Datablocksize

Column definitions	Define each column's data type, attributes, and any constraints:
	    PRIMARY KEY
	    UNIQUE
	    CHECK
	    REFERENCES
	    or GENERATED

Table-level constraints	Define multi-column constraints:
	    PRIMARY KEY
	    FOREIGN KEY
	    UNIQUE
	    CHECK conditions

Index definitions	Specify indexes for physical access to data
Row retention	COMMIT options

Figure 3.3

SPACE USAGE AND TABLE TYPES

Duplicate Row Option:

- SET
- MULITSET

Table type options:

- Permanent – This is the default.
- VOLATILE – exists only for the duration of the user's session
- GLOBAL TEMPORARY– definition is permanent, but data exists only for the duration of the user's session

Table protection options:

- [NO] FALLBACK PROTECTION
- [NO] LOG
- [NO|DUAL] BEFORE JOURNAL
- [NO|DUAL|LOCAL|[NOT] LOCAL] AFTER JOURNAL
- FREESPACE = n [PERCENT] (percentage of cylinder freespace)
- DATABLOCKSIZE = n BYTES (maximum data block size)

DataBlockSize:

For tables that are primarily used for OLTP, keep the block size small to eliminate excess I/O.

For tables that are primarily used for DSS and require full table scans, use larger block sizes.

FreeSpace:

For tables that have frequent inserts and updates, providing additional free space reduces the frequency of block splits and the resulting additional I/O. The more static a table is, the less free space is needed.

SET/MULTISET Tables

As shown above, this attribute defines duplicate row control.

A SET table cannot have duplicate rows. A MULTISET may have duplicate rows.

If there are uniqueness constraints on any column or set of columns in the table definition, or if the table has a unique index, then the table cannot have duplicate rows even if it is declared as MULTISET.

The default in ANSI mode is MULTISET. The default in Teradata mode is SET.

The ANSI SQL standard is bag (multiset)-oriented rather than set-oriented by definition. This is at odds with one of the fundamental properties of the relational model.

In relational theory, duplicate rows are not permitted. When relations are manifested physically as tables in SQL databases, duplicate rows are permitted for multiset tables only.

This is not a recommended practice: you should always either define your tables as set tables to avoid the many problems that multiset tables present or define them as multiset tables, but specify at least one of the columns to be UNIQUE NOT NULL.

Derived Temporary Tables

The semantics of derived tables are identical to those of views.

The scope of a derived table is only visible to the level of the SELECT statement calling the subquery. Derived tables are one of the options in the FROM clause, and can also be used in the ABORT, ROLLBACK, and DELETE statements.

Aggregates are not allowed in a WHERE clause predicate; however, derived tables make such calculations easy to perform. The following example shows how derived tables facilitate this.

```
SELECT last_name
      ,salary      (FORMAT '$,$$$,$99.99')
      ,avgsal      (FORMAT '$,$$$,$99.99')
 FROM
(SELECT AVG (salary) FROM employee_table)
my_temp (avgsal)
,employee_table
WHERE salary > avgsal
ORDER BY 2 DESC;


Last_name                        Salary           avgsal
--------------------         ------------      -----------
Gere                           $64,300.00       $46,879.93
Strickland                     $54,590.00       $46,879.93
Ford                           $54,590.00       $46,879.93
Student                        $48,850.00       $46,879.93
Roberts                        $48,800.00       $46,879.93
```

Figure 3.4

The (SELECT AVG (salary) FROM employee_table) functions as an INSERT INTO followed by the declaration of the derived table's name and column name(s) *my_temp (avgsal)*. There must be a one-for-one match between the projected columns in the SELECT and columns in the derived table. The derived table columns take their data type from the projected columns.

The subquery that defines the contents of a derived table cannot contain SELECT AND CONSUME requests.

You cannot specify any of the following SQL syntactical elements in a derived table:

- ORDER BY
- WITH
- WITH ... BY
- recursion

Another form of a derived table is the use of the non-recursive WITH clause. The general syntax for the WITH clause is shown in Figure 3.5.

```
WITH named_query ( columnnames )
(select expression(s)
)
<final query to show the results>;
```

Figure 3.5

The named query is similar to a derived table. The following figure is an example:

SPACE USAGE AND TABLE TYPES

```
WITH query_name(dept, totalsal) AS
(SELECT dept_no, SUM(salary)
 FROM    employee_table
 GROUP BY dept_no
)
SELECT d.dept_no AS Dept
      , TRIM(department_name) AS DeptName
      , Budget   (FORMAT '$,$$$,$$$.99') AS BudgetAmt
      , TotalSal (FORMAT '$,$$$,$$$.99') AS TotalSalaries
FROM    department_table d
JOIN    query_name
ON      d.dept_no = dept
ORDER BY 1;


  Dept  DeptName                     BudgetAmt  TotalSalaries
  ----  --------------------         ---------  -------------
   100  Marketing                  $500,000.00     $48,850.00
   200  Research and Develop       $550,000.00     $91,588.88
   300  Sales                      $650,000.00     $40,200.00
   400  Customer Support           $500,000.00    $144,180.00
```

Figure 3.6

Volatile Temporary Tables

Volatile tables do not have a persistent definition; they must be newly created each time you need to use them. The table definition is cached only for the duration of the session in which it is created.

If you frequently reuse particular volatile table definitions, consider writing a macro that contains the CREATE TABLE text for those volatile tables.

Because volatile tables are private to the session that creates them, the system does not check their creation, access, modification, and drop privileges.

The following list details the general characteristics of volatile tables:

- Both the contents and the definition of a volatile table are lost when a system reset occurs.
- Space usage is charged to the logged-in user's Spool space.
- A single session can materialize up to 1,000 volatile tables at one time.
- The primary index for a volatile table can be either an NPPI or a PPI.
- You can collect statistics on volatile table columns, including the single, multicolumn, and PARTITION column of a PPI volatile table.
- You cannot create secondary, hash, or join indexes on a volatile table.

The following options are not permitted for volatile tables:

- Referential integrity constraints
- CHECK constraints
- Permanent journaling
- Compressed column values
- DEFAULT clause
- TITLE clause
- Named indexes

Otherwise, the options for volatile tables are identical to those for global temporary tables.

SPACE USAGE AND TABLE TYPES

Temporary Table – Example

The following figures are a step-by-step example of building and utilizing a Temporary Table.

Step 1: Create the Temporary Table

```
CREATE VOLATILE TABLE dept_aggr_t
(dept_no     SMALLINT
,sum_salary  DECIMAL(10,2)
,avg_salary  DECIMAL(8,2)
,max_salary  DECIMAL(8,2)
,min_salary  DECIMAL(8,2)
,cnt_salary  INTEGER )
PRIMARY INDEX(dept_No)
ON COMMIT PRESERVE ROWS;
```

Figure 3.7

Step 2: Insert data into the Temporary Table

```
INSERT INTO Dept_Aggr_T
 SELECT Dept_no
,SUM(Salary)
, AVG(Salary)
,MAX(Salary)
,MIN(Salary)
,COUNT(Salary)
FROM Employee_Table
GROUP BY Dept_no ;
```

Figure 3.8

Step 3: Select (Join) to the Temporary Table

```
SELECT Department_Name
      ,Avg_Salary
      ,Max_Salary
      ,Min_Salary
FROM Dept_Aggr_T AS TT
INNER JOIN Department_Table D
ON TT.dept_no = D.dept_no
WHERE Cnt_Salary > 1 ;
```

Figure 3.9

Alternative CREATE TEMPORARY TABLE Option is shown below.

```
CREATE VOLATILE  TABLE Dept_Aggr_T
AS (SELECT Dept_no
,SUM(Salary) AS Sum_Salary
, AVG(Salary) AS Avg_Salary
,MAX(Salary) AS Max_Salary
,MIN(Salary) AS Min_Salary
,COUNT(Salary) AS Cnt_Salary
FROM Employee_Table
GROUP BY Dept_no )
WITH DATA
PRIMARY INDEX(dept_no)
ON COMMIT PRESERVE ROWS;
```

Figure 3.10

Global Temporary Tables

Global temporary tables have a persistent definition but do not have persistent content across sessions. The following list details the general characteristics of global temporary tables:

- Space usage is charged to the logged-in user's Temporary space.
- A single session can materialize up to 2,000 global temporary tables at one time.
- You materialize a global temporary table locally by referencing it in a data manipulation statement. To materialize a global temporary table, you must have the appropriate privilege on the base global temporary table or on the containing database or user as required by the statement that materializes the table.
- Any number of different sessions can materialize the same table definition, but the contents are different depending on the DML statements made against the individual materialized tables during the course of a session.
- The primary index for a global temporary table can be either an NPPI or a PPI.
- You cannot create a global temporary table with the ... AS ... WITH DATA. To use the ... AS ... feature to create a global temporary table, specify WITH NO DATA.

The following options are not permitted for global temporary tables:

- Referential integrity constraints
- Permanent journaling
- You can collect the following types of statistics on global temporary tables:
    - Multicolumn statistics
    - PARTITION or PARTITION#L*n* statistics
    - Sampled statistics

- You cannot create secondary, hash, or join indexes on a global temporary table

Access checking is not done on the materialized instances of any global temporary tables because those tables exist only for the duration of the session in which they are materialized.

This chart shows a comparison:

VOLATILE TABLE	GLOBAL TEMPORARY TABLE

Logon;
    Create volatile table;
    Load private data into the volatile table;
    Use the data;
    Logoff;
	Logon;
	    Create global temporary table;
	    Logoff;
	
	Now, authorized users can:
	    Logon;
	    Load private data into their materialization of the global temporary table;
	    Use their data;
	    Logoff;

Figure 3.11

SPACE USAGE AND TABLE TYPES

The following summarizes the space used by the various table types:

Table Type	Space Used	Exists
Permanent	PERMANENT	Until dropped
Derived	SPOOL	Until the end of the query
VOLATILE	SPOOL	Only for the duration of the user's session
GLOBAL TEMPORARY	TEMPORARY	Definition is permanent, but data exists only for the duration of the user's session

Figure 3.12

Queue Tables

A queue table is a special database object: a persistent table used to handle queue-oriented data, such as event processing and asynchronous data loading applications, with subsequent complex processing of the buffered data load. The properties of queue tables are similar to those of ordinary base tables, with the additional unique property of behaving like an asynchronous First-In-First-Out (FIFO) queue.

You can think of a queue table as a regular table that also has a memory-resident cache associated with it that tracks the FIFO queue ordering of its rows. Additionally, consumed rows are retrieved and deleted from the table simultaneously, which ensures that no row can be processed more than once.

Because most, if not all, rows for a given queue table are memory-resident on a PE, they are processed similarly to primary index operations made against non-queue tables, which are single-AMP operations applied with a row-hash WRITE lock on the row.

Row ordering in a queue table is not guaranteed to be truly FIFO for the following reasons:

- The system clocks on MPP system nodes are not synchronized.
- The QITS value for a row might be user-supplied or updated, either of which could change its position in the queue.
- A transaction rollback restores rows with their original QITS value, which might be an earlier value than rows that have already been consumed.
- Insert operations within the same multi-statement request might be assigned the same QITS value.

If Teradata Dynamic Workload Manager (TDWM) is enabled, one or more rules might defer consume mode operations from running. It is also true that the query scheduler might never see a queue table row because a consume mode operation might delete the row before it qualifies for a query scheduler rule. As a general rule, you should not create rules that affect SELECT AND CONSUME operations because such workload restrictions can easily lead to queue table rows being processed in an order that differs significantly from a "true" FIFO.

An ideal queue table has the following characteristics:

- Low cardinality (implying that its rows are consumed at roughly the same rate as they are inserted).
- Infrequent UPDATE operations to its rows.
- Infrequent DELETE operations on its rows.

Note: A queue table might be used to process event alerts.

When an event is detected by application code running in the database management system (such as a stored procedure), it can, for example, insert data from that incident into an event queue table by means of a trigger. An external event-processing application could then extract events from the database by submitting a SELECT AND

SPACE USAGE AND TABLE TYPES

CONSUME TOP 1 statement, which then waits for data to be inserted into a queue table.

When data arrives at the queue, the waiting SELECT AND CONSUME TOP 1 statement returns a result to the external application, which then processes the data further. The external application might then loop and submit another SELECT AND CONSUME TOP 1 statement to wait for further event data to be inserted into the queue table. This functionality eliminates the need for the polling loops required by applications, based on non-queue tables, which must blindly and repeatedly submit SELECT statements while waiting for an event to occur.

An application can perform peek, FIFO push, and FIFO pop operations on queue tables, as shown in the next chart.

TO perform a...	USE the...
FIFO push	INSERT command
FIFO pop	SELECT AND CONSUME statement
peek	SELECT statement

Figure 3.13

SYNTAX

```
CREATE [SET/MULTISET] TABLE tablename, QUEUE [ , <Create Table Options> ]
    ( QITS_column_name TIMESTAMP(6) NOT NULL
        DEFAULT CURRENT_TIMESTAMP(6)
        [ <data_attributes> <constraints> ]
    [ , <Additional Column Definitions> ] )
    <Table-level Constraints>
    <Index Definitions>;
```

Figure 3.14

The first column defined for any queue table must be a Query Insertion Timestamp (QITS) column. The system uses the QITS column to maintain the FIFO ordering of rows in the queue table. Each queue table has only one QITS column, and it must be defined with the following attributes:

column_name TIMESTAMP(6) NOT NULL DEFAULT CURRENT_TIMESTAMP(6)

The precision specification is optional for the TIMESTAMP data type specification and its DEFAULT attribute, but you cannot define either with a precision value other than 6.

The QITS column *cannot* be defined as any of the following:

- UNIQUE PRIMARY INDEX
- UNIQUE
- PRIMARY KEY
- Unique secondary index
- Identity column

The QITS column can be the NUPI for a table, but you should avoid following that practice.

Be aware that if you do not define an explicit primary index, primary key, or uniquely constrained column in the table, then the QITS column becomes its primary index by default because it is the first column defined for the table.

It might be useful to find additional queue management columns for functions such as message identification or queue sequencing.

Note: You *cannot* drop the QITS column from a queue table.

Chapter 3: Practice Questions

1. A "database full" error occurs when a database/user has consumed _____.
   a. all its allocated disk space in the system
   b. all its allocated disk space on any AMP
   c. all its allocated disk space in a cluster

2. Which of the following consume spool space?
   a. Databases
   b. Users

3. The Perm space allocated to a user or database is taken from the unallocated space of the _____.
   a. Creator
   b. Immediate owner

4. MaxSpool can be less, but never greater than, the spool limit of _____.
   a. the creator
   b. the immediate parent

5. Space accounting is maintained by _____.
   a. One PE
   b. The BYNET
   c. One AMP in the system
   d. Each AMP

6. Small block sizes are better for _____?
   a. DSS
   b. OLAP
   c. OLTP
   d. ROLAP

7. A derived table is declared in which of the following?
    a. FROM clause
    b. WHERE clause
    c. WITH ... BY ... clause

8. Which of the following cannot have statistics collected on them?
    a. Derived tables
    b. Multiset tables
    c. Queue tables
    d. Volatile tables

9. Which of the following can be used with volatile tables?
    a. Secondary indexes
    b. Join indexes
    c. Hash indexes
    d. RI constraints
    e. All of the above
    f. None of the above

10. Which of the following can be used with global temporary tables?
    a. Secondary indexes
    b. Join indexes
    c. Hash indexes
    d. RI constraints
    e. All of the above
    f. None of the above

11. Which of the following can serve as an identity column?
    a. QITS
    b. BLOB
    c. CLOB
    d. All of the above
    e. None of the above

SPACE USAGE AND TABLE TYPES

Chapter Notes

Utilize this space for notes, key points to remember, diagrams, areas of further study, etc.

Chapter 4 - SQL Optimization Strategies

Certification Objectives

- ✓ Given a scenario, identify the impact of row and set manipulation requests on application performance and on developer choices.
- ✓ Correlate BI solution development choices with data access performance.
- ✓ Describe the role of partitioning with respect to access.
- ✓ Describe the role of partitioning with respect to data integration.
- ✓ Given a scenario, select the correct Ordered Analytic Functions.
- ✓ Given a SQL request which involves date and time manipulation, identify the result.
- ✓ Given a scenario, identify the impact of NULL processing on the result set.
- ✓ Given a recursive query, identify the potential performance issues.
- ✓ Given a scenario with table definitions and SQL, identify the opportunities to collect statistics that may improve performance.

Before You Begin

You should be familiar with the following terms and concepts.

Terms	Key Concepts
Locks	The level, coverage, and persistence of each.
Lock requests	Conditions that allow or queue lock requests.
Locking modifiers	What can be changed.
Recursive queries	How are they used.
Views	When and why they should be used.
Macros	Definition and use.

Teradata 14 Solutions Development

Stored procedures	Internal vs. external.
Ordered Analytic Functions	What are they and how do they differ from normal aggregations.
Date and Time	How they are represented and handled.
Nulls	What are they and how to handle them.
Set manipulation	What are the Set operators.
Statistics	Ways they can be collected, what they should be collected on, how and when to refresh them.

Locking

Any number of users and applications can simultaneously access data stored in a Teradata Database.

The Teradata Database Lock Manager imposes concurrency control by locking the database object being accessed by each transaction and releasing those locks when the transaction either commits or rolls back its work. This control ensures that the data remains consistent for all users. Note that with the exception of pseudo-table locks, locks in the Teradata Database are not managed globally, but by each AMP individually.

Teradata locks and levels

Teradata can apply locks at the database level, the table level, or the row level. It does this by locking the 32-bit Database ID, the 32-bit Table ID, or a 32-bit Row Hash.

A lock applied to a database ID automatically locks all objects in that database. A lock applied to a table ID locks up all of the indexes and rows in that table. A lock applied to a row hash locks up all of the rows in a table having that value.

SQL OPTIMIZATION STRATEGIES

Remember, every row in the entire system is uniquely identified by the following 32-bit system values, as shown below.

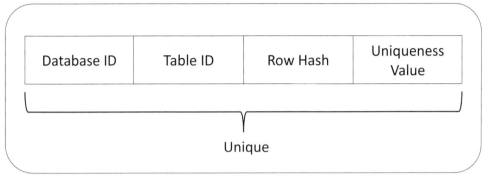

Figure 4.1

Locking strategies determine the type of object that is locked and the impact on other users, as follows:

LOCKING Strategy	Resource(s) unavailable to other users
DATABASE	All tables, views, macros and triggers owned by the database/user.
VIEW	All tables referenced in the View.
TABLE	All rows in the base table and in any secondary index and fallback subtables associated with it.
ROW	The primary copy of rows sharing the same row hash value. A row hash lock permits other users to access other data in the table and is the least restrictive type of automatic lock. A row hash lock applies to a *set* of rows that shares the same hash code. It does not necessarily, nor even generally, lock only one row. A row hash lock is applied whenever a table is accessed using a *primary index (PI)*. For an update that uses a *unique secondary index (USI)*,

LOCKING Strategy	Resource(s) unavailable to other users
	the appropriate row of the secondary index subtable is also locked. It is not necessary to lock the fallback copy of the row, nor any associated row, of a *non-unique secondary index* (NUSI) subtable.

Figure 4.2

Locks strategies and compatibility

The types of locks and their descriptions are:

LOCK TYPE	DESCRIPTION
ACCESS	Permits selection of data from a base table that is locked for write by other users. Because the data selected using an ACCESS lock can be inconsistent as the data might be modified concurrently with the request, you should only use this lock for casual inspection of data. Placing an ACCESS lock requires the SELECT privilege on the specified object.
READ	Ensures data consistency during a read operation such as a SELECT request. This is the default lock on SELECT statements. Multiple users can concurrently hold a READ lock on a base table. As long as a READ lock is in place, no modification of the object is allowed. Placing a READ lock requires the SELECT privilege on the specified object. SHARE is a synonym for READ
WRITE	Enables a single user to modify data. This is the default for INSERT, UPDATE, and DELETE statements. As long as the WRITE lock is in place, all other users

SQL OPTIMIZATION STRATEGIES

LOCK TYPE	DESCRIPTION
	are excluded from viewing or modifying the object except readers who are viewing data using an ACCESS lock. Until a WRITE lock is released, no new READ locks are permitted on the locked object. Placing a WRITE lock requires an UPDATE, INSERT, or DELETE privilege on the specified object.
EXCLUSIVE	Excludes all other users. This is the most restrictive lock. EXCLUSIVE locks are rarely used except to make structural changes to a database. This is the default on all DDL statements. Placing an EXCLUSIVE lock on a database object requires the DROP privilege on that object.
CHECKSUM	Used only with updatable cursors in embedded SQL and stored procedures.

Figure 4.3

When a lock is requested, the system will either Grant the lock, or put the request into the lock Queue as follows:

	LOCK REQUESTED			
LOCK HELD	ACCESS	READ	WRITE	EXCLUSIVE
None	Grant	Grant	Grant	Grant
ACCESS	Grant	Grant	Grant	**Queue**
READ	Grant	Grant	**Queue**	**Queue**
WRITE	Grant	**Queue**	**Queue**	**Queue**
EXCLUSIVE	**Queue**	**Queue**	**Queue**	**Queue**

Figure 4.4

Any lock can be upgraded, but only a READ lock can be downgraded to an ACCESS lock.

Locking Modifiers

Use the LOCKING modifier to change a lock. Here are the syntax formats of the LOCKING Modifier:

```
LOCKING [<table-name>] FOR <desired-locking> [NOWAIT]
LOCKING ROW FOR <desired-locking> [NOWAIT]
LOCKING DATABASE <database-name> FOR <desired-locking> [NOWAIT]
LOCKING VIEW <view-name> FOR <desired-locking> [NOWAIT]
LOCKING TABLE <table-name> FOR <desired-locking> [NOWAIT]
```

Figure 4.5

The NOWAIT Option

NOWAIT instructs the system to abort the request if the lock cannot be granted immediately. Specify this option for situations in which it is not desirable to have a request wait for resources, and possibly tie up resources another request could use, while waiting.

Recursive Queries

The WITH RECURSIVE clause defines a named query that can refer to itself in the query definition and in the SELECT statement that the WITH RECURSIVE clause precedes. The named query definition consists of at least one non-recursive, or *seed*, statement and at least one recursive statement.

The general syntax of a recursive WITH is:

```
WITH RECURSIVE named_query ( columnnames )
(<root select statement>
UNION ALL
 <recursive select statement>
)
<final query to show the results>;
```

Figure 4.6

Performance Considerations

The following broadly characterizes the performance impact of recursive query with respect to execution time:

- Using a recursive query shows a significant performance improvement over using temporary tables with a stored procedure. In most cases, there is a significant improvement.

- Using the WITH RECURSIVE clause has basically the same or equivalent performance as using the RECURSIVE VIEW.

Depth Control to Avoid Infinite Recursion

If the hierarchy is cyclic, or if the recursive statement specifies a bad join condition, a recursive query can produce a runaway query that never completes with a finite result. The best practice is to control the depth of the recursion as follows:

- Specify a depth control column in the column list of the WITH RECURSIVE clause or recursive view
- Initialize the column value to 0 in the seed statements
- Increment the column value by 1 in the recursive statements
- Specify a limit for the value of the depth control column in the join condition of the recursive statements
- Only the rows from the "immediately preceding pass" are qualified on in the current pass.

Consider the following query to create a hierarchical list of all databases. Since DBC owns DBC, this query would be infinite without the limiting AND clause.

SQL OPTIMIZATION STRATEGIES

```
WITH RECURSIVE temp_table(databasename, ownername, depth) AS
(SELECT root.databasename, root.ownername, 0 AS depth
 FROM dbc.databases root
 WHERE root.databasename = 'dbc'
 UNION ALL
 SELECT indirect.databasename, indirect.ownername,
 seed.depth + 1 AS depth
 FROM temp_table seed, dbc.databases indirect
 WHERE seed.databasename = indirect.ownername
 AND indirect.ownername <> indirect.databasename
 AND depth <= 10
)
SELECT ownername, databasename, depth
FROM temp_table
ORDER BY depth, ownername, databasename;
```

Figure 4.7

The following example uses the single-table recursion that exists in the employee_table. Employees have managers, and managers are also employees. Knowing that whoever is at the top of the hierarchy does not have a manager (currently) we start there and have the system work its way down.

```
WITH RECURSIVE query_name (employee_no, last_name, depth) AS
( SELECT root.employee_no,  root.last_name, 0 AS depth
FROM employee_table  root
WHERE root.mgr_employee_no IS NULL
UNION ALL
SELECT  indirect.employee_no,   indirect.last_name, seed.depth+1  AS depth
FROM query_name  seed, employee_table  indirect
WHERE seed.employee_no = indirect.mgr_employee_no
AND depth <= 20
)
SELECT employee_no, last_name, depth FROM query_name
ORDER BY depth;


employee_no   last_name                    depth
-----------   ------------------           -----
    1121334   Strickland                       0
    2000000   Travolta                         1
    1000234   Gere                             1
    1333454   Roberts                          1
    1324657   Willis                           2
    2312225   Mcfly                            2
    1256349   Ford                             2
    1232578   Student                          3
    2341218   Clooney                          3
```

Figure 4.8

Views

- A view is a virtual table.
- A view may define a subset of rows of a table.

SQL OPTIMIZATION STRATEGIES

- A view may define a subset of columns of a table.
- Data is neither duplicated nor stored separately for a view.
- View definitions are stored in the Data Dictionary, not in the user's own space.
- Views can join and simplify multiple tables into a single virtual table.
- Views can act as aggregated tables, where the aggregate data (sum, average, etc) is presented as the calculated results.
- A view may be a RECURSIVE view.
- Views can provide extra security by limiting the exposure of a table or tables to users accessing the data.

Recursive Views

The previous recursive WITH can be replaced with the following recursive view definition.

```
CREATE RECURSIVE VIEW query_name (employee_no, last_name, depth) AS
( SELECT root.employee_no, root.last_name, 0 AS depth
FROM employee_table root
WHERE root.mgr_employee_no IS NULL
UNION ALL
SELECT indirect.employee_no, indirect.last_name, seed.depth+1 AS depth
FROM query_name seed, employee_table indirect
WHERE seed.employee_no = indirect.mgr_employee_no
AND depth <= 20
);
```

Figure 4.9

Recommendation: Only utilities, such as FastLoad, MultiLoad, etc., should have direct access to the base tables. All other access should be done through views.

Macros

- Macros contain one or more prewritten SQL statements.
- Macros are a Teradata extension to ANSI SQL.
- Macros are stored in the Teradata Data Dictionary.
- Individual macros can be archived, copied, and restored.
- Macros can be executed from any viable SQL front-end, including:
    - SQL Assistant
    - BTEQ
    - Preprocessor
    - CLI
    - LOGON Startup
    - Another macro
- Users only need the EXEC privilege to run a macro.
- No underlying table or view privileges are required to EXECute a macro.
- The macro creator must have the necessary permissions to accomplish the SQL statements within a macro.
- Every SQL statement in a macro must end with a semicolon.
- Macros are executed as a single request. All SQL within a macro must successfully complete or any changes will be rolled back.
- Macros can provide column-level security.
- Macros can be parameterized, however, by design, they will not return parameters to the requestor.
- The *macroname* must be a unique *objectname* within the database it resides.
- Nonqualified names in a macro definition are *not* resolved in DDL statements when the macro is created. They are not resolved until the macro is performed.
- Nonqualified names in a macro definition are *fully* resolved in DML statements when the macro is created.

SQL OPTIMIZATION STRATEGIES

Macro-related commands:

COMMAND	DEFINITION
CREATE MACRO macroname AS (...) ;	Define a macro and store it the Data Dictionary.
REPLACE MACRO macroname AS (...) ;	Modify an existing macro. If the referenced macro does not exist, a new macro will be created.
EXECute macroname;	Execute the statements within the macro.
SHOW MACRO macroname;	Display a macro.
DROP MACRO macroname;	Remove a macro definition from the Data Dictionary
EXPLAIN EXEC macroname;	Display EXPLAIN text for the macro's execution.

Figure 4.10

Simple Macro Syntax

```
CREATE | REPLACE MACRO macroname
AS
( <SQL statement(s)> ) ;
```

Figure 4.11

Parameterized Macro Syntax

```
CREATE | REPLACE MACRO macroname
(parametername datatype [ , parametername datatype ... ]
AS
( <SQL statements> ) ;
```

Figure 4.12

Not all of the data attributes that can be specified for table columns can be specified in macros. For example, data type declarations and attributes have limited functionality as macro parameters. The following data attributes are never valid with macro parameters:

- CHECK constraints
- COMPRESS phrase

If a macro has multiple parameters, you must:

- Input data in the same order as specified in the macro parameter list.
- Provide the exact number of parameters specified in the list.
- Use positional commas or NULL for empty columns and filler parameters.

However, parameterized input can be scrambled in any order by including the parameter name with the value, as shown in Figure 4.13.

```
EXEC macroname (parametername3 = <value>,
parametername1 = <value>, parametername2 = <value>);
```

Figure 4.13

Stored Procedures

A stored procedure is a group of SQL, control, and condition handling statements that provides an interface to the Teradata Database. The Teradata Database also supports *external stored procedures,* which are procedures written in C, C++, or Java. A stored procedure typically consists of a procedure name, input and output parameters, and a procedure body which is stored as a database object on the Teradata Database.

In addition, a stored procedure provides multiple input / output parameters along with local variables that makes SQL a computationally complete programming language.

The Teradata Database has a table that contains the stored procedure body you create along with the compiled stored procedure object code. The Data Dictionary tables contain stored procedure parameters and attributes.

Stored procedures provide the following benefits over other embedded SQL applications:

- Reduced network traffic between the client and server providing better performance.
- Simplified maintenance because business rules are encapsulated and enforced by the database.
- Enhanced transaction control.
- Improved application security by restricting user access to procedures only as opposed to accessing data tables directly.
- Stored procedures provided better application execution because all SQL language statements are embedded and executed on the server through one CALL statement.

Nested CALL statements are treated by the PE as if they originated from the client within a stored procedure. Basically these statements will be treated as a series of implicit or explicit transactions from which they are executed.

Stored Procedures allow the combination of both SPL (Stored Procedures Language) and SQL control statements to manage the delivery and execution of the procedure.

Users can also write Stored Procedures to pass arguments that can substitute SQL syntax, including the database object names. This is called Dynamic SQL.

Macros or Stored Procedures for Tactical Queries

Macros and stored procedures now support multi-statement requests and result sets. However, because stored procedures also support conditional logic, they are typically a better choice than macros for running tactical queries.

Simple Requests

Macros or stored procedures now support the ability to run simple requests. However, stored procedures may now perform better than macros for these operations.

Multi-statement Requests

Multi-statement requests are now supported by macros and stored procedures. Therefore, performance for stored procedures and macros are now the same. In some cases, stored procedures might be better than macros.

Statements Returning Multiple Rows

Multi-statement and retuning of multi-row results sets are now allowed with stored procedures There is no longer an advantage of macros over stored procedures for returning multiple rows.

Differences between Macros and Stored Procedures

The following chart shows the differences between macros and stored procedures:

MACRO	STORED PROCEDURE
Limited procedural logic.	Advanced procedural logic.
Multi-row result sets are allowed for the same request.	Allows up to return up to 15 dynamic result sets.
Multi-statement requests are parallelized for multiple single row statements.	Utilizing the BEGIN REQUEST – END REQUEST, DYNAMIC RESULT SETS statements can be parallelized for multiple single row statements.
Stored in data dictionary.	Stored in user database.
EXPLAINs allowed.	EXPLAINs not allowed. Each stored procedure SQL statement must be EXPLAINed individually.

Figure 4.14

Variables

There are two different types of variables available for use within a stored procedure.

- Result Code Variables are status variables implicitly declared and populated by the system.
    - SQLSTATE – Receives and stores status information generated by the system after a SQL statement completes, either normally or abnormally. The information can be error or warning codes as well as information about the condition of a SQL statement. SQLSTATE is the ANSI standard.
    - SQLCODE – Receives and stores status information generated by the system after a SQL statement completes, either normally or abnormally. The information can be error or warning codes as well as information about the condition of a SQL statement. SQLSTATE is *not* ANSI standard and should not be used going forward.
    - ACTIVITY_COUNT – Holds the number of rows affected by a SQL DML statement such as Insert, Update, etc.. It can be checked after each statement completes to determine how many rows were affected for that statement.
- Host variables are used to receive values from SQL Statements (Output Variable) or to provide values to a SQL Statement (Input Variable).
- Local Variables are used within a BEGIN...END compound statement of a stored procedure. Their purpose is to hold a value between multiple statements so that the results of one SQL statement can be used in another SQL statement. Their scope is limited to the compound statement in which they were declared.

Parameters

Stored Procedures utilize Parameters to pass data between the stored procedure and the system that calls it. There are three types of parameters:

- IN - parameter used to pass data to be used during the execution of the stored procedure
- OUT - parameter used to pass data back to the "calling" system after the execution of the code within the stored procedure
- INOUT - parameter that can be used to pass data in both directions

One thing to keep in mind is that all three types of these parameters can be nullable.

Ordered Analytic Functions

Ordered analytical functions extend the Teradata Database query execution engine with the concept of an ordered set and with the ability to use the values from multiple rows in computing a new value.

The result of an ordered analytical function is handled the same as any other SQL expression. It can be a result column or part of a more complex arithmetic expression within its SELECT.

Each of the ordered analytical functions permits you to specify the sort ordering column or columns on which to sort the rows retrieved by the SELECT statement. The sort order and any other input parameters to the functions are specified the same as arguments to other SQL functions and can be any normal SQL expression.

Why Perform Ordered Analytical Calculations at the SQL Level?

Performing ordered analytical computations at the SQL level rather than through a higher level OLAP calculation engine provides four distinct advantages:

- Reduced programming effort.
- Elimination of the need for external sort routines.
- Elimination of the need to export large data sets to external tools because ordered analytical functions enable you to target the specific data for analysis within the warehouse itself by specifying conditions in the query.
- Marked enhancement of analysis performance over the slow, single-threaded operations that external tools perform on large data sets.

Teradata SQL supports two syntax alternatives for ordered analytical functions:

- ANSI SQL-2008-compliant
- Teradata

Window aggregate, rank, distribution, and row number functions are ANSI SQL-2008-compliant, while Teradata-specific functions are not.

The use of Teradata-specific functions is *strongly discouraged*. These functions are retained only for backward compatibility with existing applications.

The ordered analytic functions are:

Window aggregate functions		
AVG	REGR_AVGX	REGR_SXY
COUNT	REGR_AVGY	REGR_SYY
COVAR_POP	REGR_COUNT	STDDEV_POP
COVAR_SAMP	REGR_INTERCEPT	STDDEV_SAMP
CORR	REGR_R2	SUM

SQL OPTIMIZATION STRATEGIES

Window aggregate functions		
MAX	REGR_SLOPE	VAR_POP
MIN	REGR_SXX	VAR_SAMP
Distribution function		
PERCENT_RANK		
Rank Function		
RANK		
Row number function		
ROW_NUMBER		

Figure 4.15

Teradata SQL-specific functions (deprecated):

CSUM	MLINREG	QUANTILE
MAVG	MSUM	RANK
MDIFF		

Figure 4.16

Date/Time Manipulation

Data/Time Literals Types

Date and Time data types allow you to store date, time, and time-interval information. Below are the data types that are supported.

Data Type	Description
DATE	Special type of integer. ((YEAR - 1900) * 10000) + (MONTH * 100) + DAY Use ANSI Date form for compatibility. 4 bytes
TIME (n)	Stored as HHMMSS.nnnnnn

Data Type	Description
	6 bytes
TIMESTAMP (n)	Stored as YYMMDDHHMMSS.nnnnnn
	10 bytes
TIME (n) WITH ZONE	Stored as HHMMSS.nnnnnn+HHMM
	8 bytes
TIMESTAMP (n) WITH ZONE	Stored as YYMMDDHHMMSS.nnnnnn+HHMM
	12 bytes
INTERVAL YEAR	Used to define a field as representing a period of time in years.
INTERVAL YEAR TO MONTH	Conceptually represents a record with two fields: YEAR and MONTH. An example of *INTERVAL YEAR(3) TO MONTH* would be '114-06' which would correspond to 114 years, 6 months.
INTERVAL MONTH	Used to define a field as representing a period of time in months.
INTERVAL DAY	Used to define a field as representing a period of time in days.
INTERVAL DAY TO HOUR	Conceptually represents a record with two fields: DAY and HOUR. An example of INTERVAL DAY(3) TO HOUR would be '132 08' which would correspond to an interval of 132 days, 8 hours.
INTERVAL DAY TO MINUTE	Conceptually represents a record with three fields: DAY, HOUR, and MINUTE. An example of INTERVAL DAY(2) TO MINUTE would be '71 08:07' which would correspond to an interval of 71 days, 8 hours and 7 minutes.
INTERVAL DAY TO SECOND	Conceptually represents a record with four fields: DAY, HOUR, MINUTE and SECOND. An example of INTERVAL DAY(2) TO SECOND(3) would be '22 04:02:43.831' which would correspond to an interval of 22 days, 4 hours, 2 minutes and 43.831 seconds.

SQL OPTIMIZATION STRATEGIES

Data Type	Description
INTERVAL HOUR	Used to define a field as representing a period of time in hours.
INTERVAL HOUR TO MINUTE	Conceptually represents a record with two fields: HOUR and MINUTE. An example of INTERVAL HOUR(4) TO MINUTE would be '2947:08' which would correspond to an interval of 2947 hours and 8 minutes.
INTERVAL HOUR TO SECOND	Conceptually represents a record with three fields: HOUR, MINUTE, and SECOND. An example of INTERVAL HOUR(2) TO SECOND(3) would be '27:08:42.357' which would correspond to an interval of 27 hours, 8 minutes and 42.357 seconds.
INTERVAL MINUTE	Used to define a field as representing a period of time in minutes.
INTERVAL MINUTE TO SECOND	Conceptually represents a record with two fields: MINUTE and SECOND. An example of INTERVAL MINUTE(2) TO SECOND(0) would be '53:41' which would correspond to an interval of 53 minutes and 41 seconds.
INTERVAL SECOND	Used to define a field as representing a period of time in seconds.

Figure 4.17

The following chart describes the Temporal functions.

Function	Description		
ADD_MONTHS (d, n)	The function returns the date *d* plus the *n* months. You can use any integer for *n* months. If *d* is the last day of the month, or if the resulting month has fewer days than the day component, then the result is the last day of the resulting month. Otherwise, the result has the same day component as *d*.		
OADD_MONTHS (dtv,n)	This function is very similar to ADD_MONTHS in that it returns the date timestamp value dtv plus n months		
EXTRACT (*period* FROM *value*)	**PERIOD**	**SPECIFIES...**	
	YEAR	that the integer value for YEAR is to be extracted from the date represented by *value*.	
	MONTH	that the integer value for MONTH is to be extracted from the date represented by *value*.	
	DAY	that the integer value for DAY is to be extracted from the date represented by *value*.	
	HOUR	that the integer value for HOUR is to be extracted from the time represented by *value*.	
	MINUTE	that the integer value for MINUTE is to be extracted from the time represented by *value*.	
	SECOND	that the integer value for	

Function	Description	
		SECOND is to be extracted from the time represented by *value*.
	TIMEZONE _HOUR	that the integer value for TIMEZONE_HOUR is to be extracted from the time represented by *value*.
	TIMEZONE _MINUTE	that the integer value for TIMEZONE_MINUTE is to be extracted from the time represented by *value*.
(d1) OVERLAPS (d2)	The function determines if two time intervals overlap. Teradata SQL supports the standard SQL overlaps predicate. Each time period to the left and right of the OVERLAPS keyword is one of the following expression types: • DateTime, DateTime • DateTime, Interval • Row subquery	
LAST_DAY	Will give you the last day of the month of the given date_timestamp_value. eg: LAST_DAY('2014-02-17 01:45:22') = '2014-02-28'	
NEXT_DAY	Determines the date of the next *weekday* that is after the given date_timestamp_value. eg: NEXT_DAY('2014-05-15', 'MONDAY') = '2014-05-19'	
ROUND(DATE)	Will return the date_value with the time portion rounded to the given unit. eg: ROUND('2013-09-17', 'RM') = '2013-10-01'; ROUND('2014-07-06 12:36:45', 'Y') = '2015-01-01'. The units for rounding are the same as those used for TRUNC.	

Function	Description
TRUNC(DATE)	Will return the date_value with the time portion truncated to the given unit. eg: TRUNC('2013-09-17', 'RM') = '2013-09-01'; ROUND('2014-07-06 12:36:45', 'Y') = '2014-01-01'. The units for rounding are the same as those used for TRUNC.
MONTHS_BETWEEN	Determines the number of months between two date_time_values. eg: MONTHS_BETWEEN('2014-05-01','2014-06-03') = 1.0645…; MONTHS_BETWEEN('2014-04-17','2014-03-17') = -1

Figure 4.18

DATE FORM

DATE is supported both in its Teradata form and in the preferred ANSI DateTime form. For new development, define DATE using ANSI DATE type.

Though date values are stored as an integer, the default display of date values is controlled by the system parameter *Current DateForm*. This parameter is set by your system administrator.

DATE data can be set to be treated either using the ANSI date format (DATEFORM=ANSIDATE) or using the Teradata date format (DATEFORM=INTEGERDATE), as shown below.

SQL OPTIMIZATION STRATEGIES

Option	Description
INTEGERDATE	Sets the DATEFORM option to import and export DATE values as encoded integers. INTEGERDATE results in a default DATE format in field mode of 'YY/MM/DD' for date columns created and for date constants in character form. The 'YY/MM/DD' default DATE format can be changed by the system administrator using the tdlocaledef utility. INTEGERDATE is the default.
ANSIDATE	Sets the DATEFORM option to import and export DATE values as CHARACTER(10). Results in a 'YYYY-MM-DD' date format for date columns created and for date constants in character form.

Figure 4.19

You can see the setting of this parameter through the HELP SESSION; command.

Period Data Types

A Period represents a set of Time Granules that are contiguous within an anchored duration. The Period has an inclusive beginning bound and exclusive ending bound. For example, a period of 7 hours starting at 12:00pm would extend to 7:00pm and would include 12:00pm but not include 7:00pm.

Time Granules are those minimum segments of time that are represented by a given precision. For example, if the element type of a period is TIME(0), then the granule is one second, whereas periods with an element type of TIMESTAMP(3) will have a granule of 1 thousandth of a second.

Element Types of a Period data type are inherited from the data type of the beginning and ending elements of the Period. The element type for the beginning and ending element must be the same. The element type can be any DateTime data type including TIMESTAMP, DATE, TIME.

Data Type	Description
PERIOD(DATE)	Fixed length data type saved as two DATE values. Example: '2012-02-14, 2012-03-17'
PERIOD(TIME(n))	Fixed length data type saved as two TIME values. Example: '07:32:14.864, 12:19:52.004'
PERIOD(TIME(n) WITH TIME ZONE)	Fixed length data type saved as two TIME WITH TIME ZONE values. Example: '14:34:12.864-08:00, 18:39:51.464-08:00'
PERIOD(TIMESTAMP(n))	Fixed length data type saved as two TIMESTAMP values. Example: ' 2012-02-14 07:32:14.864, 2012-03-17 12:19:52.004'
PERIOD(TIMESTAMP(n) WITH TIME ZONE)	Fixed length data type saved as two TIME WITH TIME ZONE values. Example: ' 2012-02-14 14:34:12.864-08:00, 2012-03-17 18:39:51.464-08:00'

Figure 4.20

Period Manipulation

There are many functions and operators for manipulating and/or evaluating Period values. A few of the more common ones are:

Function/Operator	Description
BEGIN	Returns the beginning bound of a period_value_expression. eg: BEGIN('2014-01-02', '2014-01-05') = '2014-01-02'
END	Returns the ending bound of a period_value_expression. eg: BEGIN('2014-01-02', '2014-01-05') = '2014-01-05'
CONTAINS	Predicate used to determine if one period_value_expression is wholly contained within another period_value_expression. eg; ('2013-12-15', '2014-03-10')CONTAINS('2014-01-02', '2014-01-05') = TRUE
LAST	Returns the last value of the Period. In other words, it takes the ending bound and subtracts one *granule* of the element type. eg: LAST('2014-06-15', '2014-09-10') = '2014-09-09';
NEXT	Returns the next succeeding value of the Period. eg: NEXT('2014-04-05', '2014-06-21') = '2014-06-22'
OVERLAPS	Predicate used to determine if one period_value_expression overlaps another period_value_expression. eg; ('2013-12-15', '2014-03-10')OVERLAPS('2014-01-02', '2014-01-05') = TRUE; ('2014-02-19', '2014-03-10')OVERLAPS('2014-03-02', '2014-07-05') = TRUE

Figure 4.21

Calendar Functions

Teradata has many built in functions for working with calendar information.

Function	Description
td_day_of_week	Returns the integer value for the day of the week, where Sunday = 1.
td_day_of_month	Returns the integer value for the number of days (up to 31) from the first day of the month through the specified date.
td_day_of_year	Returns the integer value for the number of days (up to 365) from the first day of the year(Jan. 1) through the specified date.
td_day_of_calendar	Returns the integer value for the number of days from 01/01/1900 through the specified date.
td_weekday_of_month	Returns the integer value for the nth incidence (up to 5) of the weekday for the given date.
td_week_of_month	Returns the integer value for the nth full week since the start of the month for the given date. The first partial week, if there is one, is Week 0.
td_week_of_year	Returns the integer value for the nth full week since the start of the year (Jan.1) for the given date. The first partial week, if there is one, is Week 0.
td_week_of_ calendar	Returns the integer value for the nth full week since 01/01/1900 for the given date. The first partial week, if there is one, is Week 0.
td_month_of_quarter	Returns an integer value representing which month of a quarter it is for a

SQL OPTIMIZATION STRATEGIES

Function	Description
	specified date.
td_month_of_year	Returns an integer value representing the number of months from the start of the year through a specified date.
td_month_of_ calendar	Returns an integer value representing the number of months since 01/01/1900 through a specified date.
td_quarter_of_year	Returns an integer value representing which quarter of a year it is for a specified date.
td_quarter_of_ calendar	Returns an integer value representing the number of quarters since 01/01/1900 through a specified date.
td_year_of_calendar	Returns the year for the given date.

Figure 4.22

Business Calendars

Teradata comes with three system-defined business calendars. All three are based on the Gregorian calendar and have 365 days for all years except leap years which have 366 days. The three calendars supplied with Teradata are:

- ISO
- COMPATIBLE
- TERADATA

The default calendar for a session is the Teradata calendar but you can set your session to be one of the other business calendars with the SET SESSION CALENDAR command.

Differences in the Calendars

- **ISO** - This calendar is based on European and ISO standard where the first week of the year is the first week that has at least 4 days. The first day of a week is Monday.
- **COMPATIBLE** – This calendar is compatible with Oracle and dictates that the first full week of the year begins on Jan. 1 regardless of what day of the week it is. The first day of the week can change from one year to the next.
- **Teradata** – The first full week of the year starts on the first Sunday of the year. For years where Jan. 1 is on a day other than Sunday, those days prior to the first Sunday belong to Week 0.

Nulls

Nulls are neither values nor do they signify values; they represent the unknown values. A null is a place holder indicating that no value is present.

You *cannot* solve for the value of a null because, by definition, it *has* no value. For example, the expression NULL = NULL has no meaning and therefore can never be true. A query that specifies the predicate WHERE NULL = NULL is not valid because it can never be true. The meaning of the comparison it specifies is not only unknown, but unknowable.

These properties make the use and interpretation of nulls in SQL problematic. The following sections outline the behavior of nulls for various SQL operations to help you understand how to use them in data manipulation statements and to interpret the results those statements affect.

Nulls and DateTime and Interval Data

A DateTime or Interval value is either atomically null or it is not null. For example, you cannot have an interval of YEAR TO MONTH in which YEAR is null and MONTH is not.

Result of Expressions That Contain Nulls

Here are some general rules for the result of expressions that contain nulls:

- When any component of a value expression is null, then the result is null.
- The result of a conditional expression that has a null component is unknown.
- If an operand of any *arithmetic* operator (such as + or -) or function (such as ABS or SQRT) is null, then the result of the operation or function is null with the exception of ZEROIFNULL. If the argument to ZEROIFNULL is NULL, then the result is 0.
- COALESCE, a special shorthand variant of the CASE expression, returns NULL if all its arguments evaluate to null. Otherwise, COALESCE returns the value of the first non-null argument.

Nulls and Comparison Operators

If either side of an operand is null, then the result is unknown. If either operand is the keyword NULL, an error is returned that recommends using IS NULL or IS NOT NULL instead. The following examples indicate this behavior.

    5 = NULL
    5 <> NULL
    NULL = NULL
    NULL <> NULL

5 = NULL + 5

Instead of using comparison operators, use the IS NULL operator to search for fields that contain nulls and the IS NOT NULL operator to search for fields that do not contain nulls.

Using IS NULL is different from using the comparison operator =. When you use an operator like =, you specify a comparison between values or value expressions, whereas when you use the IS NULL operator, you specify an existence condition.

Nulls and CASE Expressions

The following rules apply to nulls and CASE expressions:

- CASE and its related expressions COALESCE and NULLIF can return a null.
- NULL and null expressions are not valid in a CASE test expression in the valued CASE form.
- When testing for NULL, it is best to use a searched CASE expression using the IS NULL or IS NOT NULL operators in the WHEN clause.
- NULL and null expressions are valid as THEN clause conditions.

Excluding Nulls

To exclude nulls from the results of a query, use the operator IS NOT NULL.

Null Sorts as the Lowest Value in a Collation

When you use an ORDER BY clause to sort records, Teradata Database sorts null as the lowest value. Sorting nulls can vary from RDBMS to RDBMS. Other systems may sort null as the highest value.

SQL OPTIMIZATION STRATEGIES

If any row has a null in the column being grouped, then all rows having a null are placed into one group.

Nulls and Aggregate Functions

With the important exception of COUNT(*), aggregate functions ignore nulls in their arguments. This treatment of nulls is very different from the way arithmetic operators and functions treat them.

This behavior can result in apparent non-transitive anomalies. For example, if there are nulls in either column A or column B (or both), then the following expression is virtually always true.

$$SUM(A) + (SUM\ B) <> SUM\ (A+B)$$

In other words, for the case of SUM, the result is never a simple iterated addition if there are nulls in the data being summed.

The only exception to this is the case in which the values for columns A and B are *both* null in the same rows, because in those cases the entire row is disregarded in the aggregation. This is a trivial case that does not violate the general rule.

The same is true, the necessary changes being made, for all the aggregate functions except COUNT(*).

If this property of nulls presents a problem, you can always do either of the following workarounds, each of which produces the desired result of the aggregate computation SUM(A) + SUM(B) = SUM(A+B).

- Always define NUMERIC columns as NOT NULL DEFAULT 0.
- Use the NULLIF or ZEROIFNULL functions within the aggregate function to convert any nulls to zeros for the computation, for example:

SUM(NULLIF(x,x) + NULLIF(y,y)
SUM(ZEROIFNULL(x) + ZEROIFNULL(y))

COUNT(*) *does* include nulls in its result, since it is a count of physical rows.

Row vs. Set Manipulation

The SELECT statement returns an answer *set* from the rows it processes. One query = one answer *set*.

The set operator(s) let you combine the results from two or more SELECT statements to construct more complex queries. Teradata supports three classes of set operations:

- UNION [DISTINCT] and UNION ALL
- INTERSECT [DISTINCT] and INTERSECT ALL
- EXCEPT [DISTINCT] or MINUS [DISTINCT] and EXCEPT ALL, MINUS ALL

By default, duplicate rows are not returned by any of the Set operators.

Note: To permit duplicate rows to be returned, specify the ALL option.

Set Operations – Restrictions

SQL statements that contain set operators are called compound queries. In order for a compound query to work successfully, the following conditions must exist:

- The result sets of both queries must have the same number of columns.
- The corresponding columns in the queries must have the same data type or must be implicitly convertible to the same data type.
- If the names of the columns match, SQL uses that column name in the answer set.
- If the column names are different, SQL uses the names from the first query in the set operation. Use an AS clause in the first query if you want to rename a column.
- The data type, title, and format clauses contained in the first SELECT statement determine the data type, title, and format information that appear in the final result.
- You can specify an optional ORDER BY clause only in the final query in the set statement. SQL applies the sort to the final combined result.
- You can specify GROUP BY and HAVING only in individual queries. You cannot use them to affect the result.

UNION

The UNION operation combines the results of two subqueries into a single result that consists of all of the rows from both queries.

INTERSECT

The INTERSECT operator combines the results of two queries into a single result set that consists of only the common rows they share.

EXCEPT/MINUS

The EXCEPT (ANSI) or MINUS (Teradata) operation returns only the rows that are unique to the first query, removing any rows that it has in common with the second query.

Multiple Set Operators and Precedence Order

If multiple operators appear in the same query, the SQL executes them from left to right. INTERSECT, however takes higher precedence will be done first before all other Operators, unless parentheses specify a different order.

For example, consider the following example:

```
SELECT statement_1
UNION
SELECT statement_2
EXCEPT
SELECT statement_3
INTERSECT
SELECT statement_4;
```

Figure 4.23

The operations are performed in the following order:

1. Intersect the results of statement_3 and statement_4.
2. Union the results of statement_1 and statement_2.
3. Subtract the intersected rows from the union.

You can use set operators within the following operations:

- Simple queries
- Derived tables
- Subqueries

SQL OPTIMIZATION STRATEGIES

- INSERT ... SELECT clauses
- View definitions

SELECT statements connected by set operators can include all of the normal clause options for SELECT except the WITH clause.

Set operations do not operate on SELECT AND CONSUME statements. In addition, you cannot use set operators with CLOB or BLOB types.

The following restrictions apply to UDT types involved in set operations:

- Multiple UDTs involved in set operations must be identical types because Teradata Database does not perform implicit type conversion on UDTs involved in set operations.
  A workaround for this restriction is to use CREATE CAST to define casts that cast between the UDTs and then explicitly invoke the CAST function within the set operation.
- UDTs involved in set operations must have ordering definitions.

Teradata Database generates ordering functionality for distinct UDTs where the source types are not LOBs. To create an ordering definition for structured UDTs or distinct UDTs where the source types are LOBs, or to replace system-generated ordering functionality, use CREATE ORDERING.

Collect Statistics

Statistics are a critical component in ensuring the Optimizer chooses a good query plan when SQL statements are submitted for processing. There are four approaches to collecting statistics which are as follows:

- Random (Dynamic) AMP Sampling (database performed)

- Full statistics collection
- Using the SAMPLE option
- SUMMARY option

Collecting stats provides the Optimizer with a row count in the table(s) being queried. The Optimizer will then utilize this information to determine the best way to access the data. The additional benefits of collecting stats are as follows:

- If your data distribution is uneven, then stats can improve performance in accessing a column or index data during a query operation.
- Statistics provide the Optimizer the ability to use secondary, hash, or join indexes as opposed to doing full-table scans in queries.
- Provide performance benefits when doing complex queries and join operations.
- Improve the estimates of intermediate spool files based on the conditions specified in an SQL query. This is critical for determining join order for tables along with identifying the type of join to best resolve query.
- Empower the Optimizer to take advantage of NUSI Bit Mapping when available.
- Statistics information remains intact during reconfiguration operations.

Collect Statistics Process

During the stats collection process, Teradata will collect and process data demographic information on each AMP. Once complete, this information is sent to one AMP in order to merge, sort, and distribute the data based on the frequency into as many as 500(default 250) intervals.

SQL OPTIMIZATION STRATEGIES

Based on the distribution and the degree of skew in the data for each column, different histogram options can be utilized to determine cardinality and statistics.

Equally distributed and height interval histogram.

This means that each of the 250 intervals has the same number of values. For this to happen, the widths in the intervals must vary.

250 equal-height intervals in the histogram.

This states that intervals represent a percentile for the values it represents. For each column, statistics are expressed as an equal-height no skewing interval histogram if the frequencies of its values are normally distributed.

Each interval consists of roughly 1% of the table rows. The information gathered on the table consists of the following:

- Most frequent data value for the column or index
- Number of rows with the most frequent data value
- Number of data values not equal to the most frequent data value
- Number of rows not equal to the most frequent data value
- The minimum data value for the table
- Number of NULLs

Statistics Considerations

You can collect or refresh statistics on a combined maximum of 512 columns and indexes. Even though this feature may consume more system resources to complete, the benefit is that the Optimizer has better information. The end result is more efficient execution plans, which will reduce system resource consumption during query processing.

The use of statistics assists the Optimizer in making better execution plans. However, collecting statistics on columns not utilized in queries consumes unnecessary resources with no performance gains.

There are five primary areas in which statistics should be collected:

- Tables
- Columns
- Multi-Columns
- Indexes
- Partitions

It is recommended that you collect at the column level because indexes can be dropped and recreated quite often. Multi-column stats can be done at the column level without creating an index first.

In order to collect statistics, you will need the INDEX privilege. Single column stats (whether index or not) are always stored in DBC.TVFields whereas multi-column stats (indexed or not) are always stored in DBC.Indexes.

Note: Statistics can be collected on Global Temporary Tables. However, when users logoff; the data in these tables will be deleted along with the statistics.

Multi-Column Statistics Considerations

If a frequently used access path (indexed or not) consists of multiple ANDed columns, collecting statistics on the individual columns will not help the Optimizer. The optimizer needs to know what the combined mix of values looks like.

ANDed secondary index columns may qualify for NUSI Bit Mapping with individual statistics being available.

SQL OPTIMIZATION STRATEGIES

Random AMP Sampling

Dynamic Sampling gathers information from an AMP which is selected from the Table ID. Basically, this means that different AMPs will be assigned to gather sample information for different tables. This guarantees no single AMP will be overloaded with sampling requests.

Since this process only uses a single AMP, you need to be aware that if the data is not distributed evenly, the Optimizer could make improper choices. In all cases, the Optimizer will choose a conservative path to process queries when this technique is deployed.

It is possible to randomly sample table rows from more than a single AMP. The number of randomly selected AMPs from which the system samples statistics is controlled by an internal flag. The default is one AMP, but it is possible to change this default specification to sample statistics from 2 AMPs, 5 AMPs, all AMPs in a node, or all AMPs on your system. Another internal flag controls the percentage of rows to read.

Because of multiple AMP sampling, the Optimizer will receive better estimates with which to generate a query plan. This new option will improve tables with heavily skewed data. Keep in mind that the more AMPs sampled, the better will be the estimates.

Data Dictionary Cache

The dictionary cache is a buffer in parsing engine memory that stores the most recently used dictionary information. These entries, which also contain statistical information used by the Optimizer, are used to convert database object names to their numeric IDs.

Caching the information reduces I/O activity for the following items:

- Resolving database object names

- Optimizing access paths
- Validating access rights

When the Parser needs definitions not found in cache, it asks an AMP to retrieve the necessary information. When the information is received, the Parser stores it in the dictionary cache. If another SQL statement requires information about the same database object, the Parser retrieves it from cache rather than performing the more costly task of asking the AMP multiple times for the same information.

If an SQL statement changes the contents of the data dictionary, a spoil message is sent to every PE, instructing them to drop the changed definitions from their respective dictionary caches. The dictionary cache is purged periodically in anticipation that query plans based upon sampled stats become old over time, forcing new samples to occur.

Full Statistics

A full COLLECT STATISTICS statement is the most complete method of gathering demographic information about a column or an index. Below are the benefits:

- Best option for columns or indexes where data is highly skewed
- Recommended for small tables, with fewer than 100 rows per AMP
- Columns where the number of distinct values is moderate or low
- For all NUSIs and other access columns used with queries
- Statistics on a column or index are either sampled or full, but not both. The most recent COLLECT STATISTICS determines if it is sampled or full.
- For all columns/indexes where the USING SAMPLE does not provide accurate estimates.

SQL OPTIMIZATION STRATEGIES

In order to get as accurate a row count as possible, the more extensive dynamic AMP sampling approach, which samples all AMPs, is used by default for volatile tables.

Because tables are in a constant state of change, it is up to the administrator to keep collected statistics refreshed. It is common practice for many Teradata sites to re-collect statistics on the majority of their tables, or partitions, when they change by 10%.

In addition, because of the statistics options now available, it is recommended that you take some time and effort to determine the best options that provide the optimal results.

Sample Statistics

Full table statistics requires scanning the base table in order to sort and calculate the number of occurrences for each distinct value. The process in some cases can be time consuming and the resources required to collect and refresh statistics can create problems especially on large tables.

Using the sample option reduces the resources and time required to perform statistics collection. However, this should not be utilized as a replacement for full statistics collection. It is recommended that analysis and planning should be conducted before or when utilizing this option.

Sampling is recommended for the following:

- Large tables
- When resource consumption from the collection process is a serious performance or cost concern

Sampling is not recommended for the following:

- Small tables

- To replace all existing full scan collections
- If the system does not determine the correct sample size which will impact accurate statistics
- Statistics on a column or index are either sample or full. It cannot be both, and when you refresh statistics, the system will determine if the stats are sample or full
- Do not use sampling with highly skewed data

Note: This feature cannot be utilized on global temporary tables or to join indexes.

The performance enhancement gained by sampling a portion, rather than all, of table data is offset by decreased confidence in the accuracy of the statistics.

When you use sampled statistics rather than full-table statistics, you are trading time in exchange for less accurate statistics. The underlying premise for using sampled statistics is nothing more than the assumption that sampled statistics are better than no statistics.

All existing statistics can be refreshed in a single command, by not specifying any INDEX or COLUMN entries.

COLLECT STATISTICS - Recommendations

Here are some excellent guidelines on what you should collect statistics on:

- **Non-unique Secondary Indices (NUSI):** It is very important to collect statistics on all NUSIs because this will impact whether or not the optimizer chooses to use the NUSI, which could result in substantial differences in query run times. If the NUSI is used in the ORDER BY command, it is important to collect statistics on this column. This will enable the optimizer

SQL OPTIMIZATION STRATEGIES

to accurately compare the cost of using that index versus using a different access path.

- **Unique Primary Indices (UPI)**: It is important to collect statistics on a UPI if the table is small (less than 100 rows per AMP) and if no other statistics are collected on that table. The only way the optimizer knows how many rows are in the table is by collecting statistics on the primary index. This is an additional reason to collect UPI statistics. If there are multiple tables to be joined in a query, the optimizer can produce better join plans if you have PI statistics for each table.

- **Non-unique Primary Indices (NUPI):** Statistics should always be collected. As noted above, if there are multiple tables to be joined in a query, the optimizer can produce better join plans if you have PI statistics for each table.

- **Join Indexes:** Statistics should be collected separately for base table columns and join index columns. The statistics for base tables and join indexes are not interchangeable, and the demographics for values in a base table are typically different from the join index values. Statistics for a join index should always be collected on the primary index column(s) of the join index. If there is a secondary index on the join index, then it is useful to collect statistics on the column(s) used to define that secondary index. In addition, it is a good practice to collect statistics on columns used as search condition, columns used to join a join index with a table that is not part of the join index, and other popular join index columns, like those used frequently in WHERE conditions.

- **Hash Indexes:** Column statistics for single-table join indexes and hash indexes are often best collected directly on the base table columns rather than separately as is always required for multiple table join indexes.

- **Join Columns:** It is highly recommended to collect statistics on columns used in table joins. It is even more important to collect stats on columns involved in joining more than two tables. In addition, it makes sense to collect statistics on all columns of small reference tables used in joins. This will assist the optimizer in determining the best method and order for joining the tables together. Lastly, statistics helps the Optimizer to estimate with high confidence the spool file size required for the result set.

- **Partition Columns:** It is important to realize that the Optimizer uses statistics to estimate cardinalities and selectivities, not to determine whether a partition is populated with rows, and this applies equally to PPI and NPPI tables regarding PARTITION statistics. This judgment cannot be made from evaluating standard data statistics and demographics. You should collect single-column PARTITION statistics to enable the Optimizer to take advantage of the more accurate PPI costing made possible when PARTITION statistics exist.

- **Qualifying Columns:** Any column used in a WHERE clause is a candidate for statistics collection. In particular, it is vital to collect statistics on columns containing highly skewed data. The reason for this is that when there are no statistics on a skewed column, the optimizer chooses to take a conservative course by assuming that a certain percentage of the data values will qualify for the query.

Note: Accurate statistics could make the difference between a successful query and a query that runs out of spool space.

You can collect statistics on a group of non-indexed columns. Collecting statistics on a group of columns allows the Optimizer to better estimate the number of rows required to complete queries.

In addition, this feature saves overhead cost because you no longer have to use a secondary index in order to collect statistics on a group of columns. The benefits here are space savings and I/O overhead because you no longer need to create secondary indexes for just that purpose.

The recommendation is to collect statistics on a group of non-indexed columns based on the following:

- They appear frequently together in query selection conditions.
- A secondary index is defined solely to allow statistics collection and is never used for indexed data access.
- The Optimizer's row estimate in the EXPLAIN output is incorrect which results in a bad query plan. Collecting stats on the group of columns in this query can definitely improve performance.

You should consider collecting statistics on the following to help make certain the best query plans:

- All indexes.
- Join columns that are used often.
- Columns that are frequently referenced in WHERE clause predicates, particularly if those columns contain skewed data and the columns are not indexed.
- The partitioning column set of a row-partitioned table.
- The system-defined PARTITION column for all tables: NoPI, PPI, NPPI, Column-Partitioned.

Chapter 4: Practice Questions

1. The lowest level of locking in Teradata is the _____.
   a. Table
   b. Individual row
   c. Row hash

2. Which of the following locks can be downgraded?
   a. Exclusive
   b. Write
   c. Read
   d. Access

3. How many DDL statements can appear in a macro?
   a. One
   b. Two
   c. Three

4. Generally speaking, which of the following performs best?
   a. Macros
   b. Stored Procedures

5. Which of the following can be EXPLAINed?
   a. Macros
   b. Stored Procedures
   c. Both

6. Which of the following analytic functions have been deprecated and should not be used? (choose 3)
   a. SUM
   b. CSUM
   c. MSUM
   d. AVG
   e. MAVG

7. In an ORDER BY, nulls always sort _____.
    a. low
    b. high

8. Which of the set operators return duplicate rows by default?
    a. UNION
    b. INTERSECT
    c. EXCEPT
    d. All of the above
    e. None of the above

9. Unless parentheses indicate a different order, which set operator takes a higher precedence?
    a. UNION
    b. INTERSECT
    c. EXCEPT

Chapter Notes

Utilize this space for notes, key points to remember, diagrams, areas of further study, etc.

Chapter 5 - Indexes

Certification Objectives

- ✓ Given a scenario, identify the behavior of an identity column.
- ✓ Given a scenario with table definitions and SQL, identify the opportunities to create secondary indexes that may improve performance.
- ✓ Given a scenario with table definitions and SQL, identify the opportunities to create join indexes that may improve performance.
- ✓ Given a scenario with table definitions, SQL, and data demographics, identify the best performing partitioning definition.

Before You Begin

You should be familiar with the following terms and concepts:

Terms	Key Concepts
Primary Index	Unique or non-unique row distribution index.
Secondary Indexes	USI, NUSI, Bit Mapping for access.
VOSI and Hash NUSI	How do they differ from normal NUSIs.
PPI/MLPPI	CASE_N, RANGE_N, NO CASE, NO RANGE, UNKNOWN partitioning.
Vertical/Horizontal Table Partitioning	How each can be accomplished.
Join Indexes	What are the three basic types.
Sparse Indexes	Where are they most useful.
Identity column	System generated unique identifier.

PI/SI Access Chart

The figure below shows an overview of accessing a table either by its PI or by a Secondary Index or no index.

SINGLE TABLE CASE

WHERE   Table_1.Col_1 = :value_1
  AND   Table_1.Col_2 = :value_2 ;

Col_1 \ Col_2	USI	NUSI	NOT INDEXED
UPI	Col_1	Col_1	Col_1
NUPI	note 1	Col_1	Col_1
USI	Either	Col_1	Col_1
NUSI	Col_2	note 2	note 3
NOT INDEXED	Col_2	note 3	FTS

Column the Optimizer uses for access

Notes

1. The Optimizer prefers Unique indexes (Col_2). Only one row is involved, though it is a two-AMP operation.

    It chooses the NUPI (Col_1) only if its selectivity is close to a UPI.

2. Depending on relative selectivity, the Optimizer chooses Col_1, Col_2, NUSI Bit Mapping of Col_1 and Col_2, or a FTS.

3. It depends on the selectivity of the index.

Figure 5.1

NUSI Bitmapping

When statistics have been collected on NUSI indexed columns, the Optimizer might consider using a NUSI Bit Mapping operation in its query plan. NUSI Bit Mapping is a mechanism that intersects the data values to determine if common Row IDs exist between multiple NUSI values. When the query utilizes several weakly-selected indexes that are strongly selecting together, the Optimizer will most likely choose a NUSI Bit Mapping operation, which reduces the number of base rows that are accessed in the result set.

This approach can achieve significant performance improvement, because it reduces the number of base table I/Os and is much faster than copying, sorting, and comparing the Row ID lists.

At least two NUSI equality conditions are required in order for NUSI Bit Mapping to be considered. In addition, all NUSIs in the query must be linked together using the AND operator. Finally, all of the conditions in the WHERE/AND clause must yield an amount of rows that is less than one row per data block.

When WHERE conditions are connected by a logical OR, the Optimizer typically performs a full-table scan and applies the ORed conditions to every row without considering an index.

Strongly selective NUSI = Rows/Value < Data Blocks/AMP

A weakly selective NUSI accesses one or more rows per data block. If all of the data blocks would have to be accessed, the Parser will ignore the NUSI (and its processing overhead) and do a full-table scan.

Weakly selective NUSI = Rows/Value >= 1 Data Block/AMP

Note: Any OR operators in the query will almost always result in the Optimizer choosing a full table scan. You can determine if a query utilizes NUSI Bit Mapping by performing an EXPLAIN on the query

The following chart explains the Optimizer's evaluation and choice:

IF all conditions are ANDed together and ...	AND their composite selectivity is ...	THEN the Optimizer ...
one index is strongly selective		selects it alone and applies the remaining constraints to the selected rows as residual constraints.
all of the indexes are weakly selective	also weakly selective	performs a full-table scan and applies the conditions to every row.
all of the indexes are weakly selective	strongly selective	can instruct each AMP to construct bit maps to determine which ROWIDs their local NUSI rows have in common and then access just those rows, applying the conditions to them exclusively.

Figure 5.2

Value-Ordered NUSI

Normally, index rows of a NUSI are stored in row hash order. For this reason, queries doing a range check may require a FTS of the NUSI sub-table to find the ROWIDs for the base table. An option exists that allows one to have the system store the NUSI rows in value order, thereby avoiding a FTS of the NUSI in favor of range access.

An option exists that allows you to have the system store the index rows in order of their data value, thereby making queries over a *range* of values using the NUSI possible. Use EXPLAIN to verify this is happening as expected. Be certain to COLLECT STATISTICS on your indexes.

Note: For most applications, a partitioned primary index on a join index is a better choice to handle range conditions than is a value-ordered NUSI.

Value-ordered NUSIs have the following limitations:

- The sort key is limited to a single numeric or DATE column.
- The sort key column cannot exceed four bytes in length.
- If defined over multiple columns and with an ORDER BY clause, they count as two consecutive indexes against the total of 32 non-primary indexes you can define on a base or join index table. One index represents the column list and the other index represents the ordering column.

The system automatically assigns incrementally increasing numbers to indexes when they are created on a table. This is not important externally except for the case of composite value-ordered NUSIs, because these indexes not only consume two of the allotted 32 index numbers from the pool, but those two index numbers are *consecutive*.

To understand why this is important, consider the following scenario:

- You create 32 indexes on a table, none of which is value-ordered.
- You drop every other index on the table. For example, if you had dropped all the even-numbered indexes, there would now be 16 odd-numbered index numbers available to be assigned to indexes created in the future.
- You attempt to create a value-ordered multicolumn NUSI.
- The request aborts and the system returns an error message to you.

The reason the request aborts is that two *consecutive* index numbers were not available for assignment to the composite value-ordered NUSI.

You are still able to create 16 additional non-value-ordered NUSIs, single-column value-ordered NUSIs, USIs, hash indexes, or join indexes, but you cannot create any composite value-ordered NUSIs.

Hash NUSI

Hash Indexes are very similar to both single-table join and Secondary Indexes. From an architectural standpoint, Hash Indexes incorporate the use of auxiliary structures that are transparently embedded in the Hash Index column. These auxiliary structures are components of the base table, and are added to the Hash Index definition by default. This process distinctly distinguishes Hash Indexes from single-table Join Indexes.

Hash Indexes are similar to secondary indexes in the following ways:

- Created for a single table only.

- The CREATE syntax is simple and very similar to a Secondary Index.
- May cover a query without access of the base table rows.
- Hash Indexes are always compressed with the column list being field 1.

Hash Indexes are like Join Indexes in the following ways:

- They "pre-locate" joinable rows to a common location.
- The distribution and sequencing of the rows is user specified.
- Very similar to single-table Join Index.
- A table with a trigger cannot also have a Join Index or a Hash Index.

Hash Indexes are unlike Join Indexes in the following ways:

- No aggregation operators are permitted.
- They are always defined on a single table.
- No secondary indexes may be built on the Hash Index.
- Automatically contains base table PI value as part of Hash Index sub-table row.

When queries contain columns referenced and defined in Hash Index, this will enable the Optimizer to cover the query rather than access its underlying base table.

It is worth noting that query covering can be accomplished by Secondary Indexes as well, but a Hash Index is better when there is a requirement for a wider range of query processing. However, because Hash Indexes have more overhead than Secondary Indexes, the recommendation is to not define them on a table when a Secondary Index would serve the same purpose.

Hash Indexes vs. Single-Table Join Indexes

The reasons for using hash indexes are similar to those for using single-table join indexes. Not only can hash indexes optionally be specified to be distributed in such a way that their rows are AMP-local with their associated base table rows, but they can also provide a transparent direct access path to those base table rows to complete a query only partially covered by the index.

This facility makes Hash indexes somewhat similar to secondary indexes in function. Hash indexes are also useful for covering queries so that the base table need not be accessed at all. The most apparent external difference between hash and single-table join indexes is in the syntax of the SQL statements used to create them. The syntax for CREATE HASH INDEX is similar to that for CREATE INDEX. As a result, it is simpler to create a hash index than to create a functionally comparable single-table join index.

The following list summarizes the similarities of hash and single-table join indexes:

- Primary function of both is to improve query performance.
- Both are maintained automatically by the system when the relevant columns of their base table are updated by a DELETE, INSERT, or UPDATE statement.
- Both can be the object of any of the following SQL statements.
    - COLLECT STATISTICS (Optimizer Form)
    - DROP STATISTICS (Optimizer Form)
    - HELP INDEX
- Both receive their space allocation from permanent space and are stored in distinct tables.
- Both can be hash- and value-ordered.
- Both can be FALLBACK protected.
- Neither can be queried or directly updated.
- Neither can store an arbitrary query result.

- Neither can be used to partially cover a query that contains a TOP *n* or TOP *m* PERCENT clause.
- Neither can be defined using the system-derived PARTITION column.
- Both share the same restrictions for use with the MultiLoad, FastLoad, TPT, and Archive/Recovery utilities.

The following table summarizes the differences between hash and join indexes:

HASH INDEX	JOIN INDEX
Indexes one table only.	Can index multiple tables.
A logical row corresponds to one and only one row in its referenced base table.	A logical row can correspond to either of the following, depending on how the join index is defined: • One and only one row in the referenced base table. • Multiple rows in the referenced base tables.
Column list cannot contain aggregate or ordered analytical functions.	Column list can contain aggregate functions.
Cannot have a secondary index.	Can have a secondary index.
Supports transparently added, system-defined columns that point to the underlying base table rows.	Does not add underlying base table row pointers implicitly. Pointers to underlying base table rows can be created explicitly by defining one element of the column list using the keyword ROWID.
Primary index cannot be partitioned.	Primary index of noncompressed forms can be partitioned.
Cannot be defined on a table that also has triggers.	Can be defined on a table that also has triggers.

HASH INDEX	JOIN INDEX
Compression, if used, is added transparently by the system with no user input.	Compression, if used, is explicitly specified in the CREATE JOIN INDEX request by the user.

Figure 5.3

PPI - Partitioned Primary Index

Partitioning of a table can be accomplished through the CREATE TABLE or ALTER TABLE commands.

You can define both single-level and multi-level PPIs for global temporary and volatile tables, for standard base tables (but not queue tables), and for non-compressed join indexes.

When a table or join index is created with a PPI, its rows are hashed to the appropriate AMPs and then assigned to their computed internal partition number based on the value of a partitioning expression defined by the user when the table was created or altered. Once assigned to a partition, the rows are stored in row hash order.

The partitioning columns do not have to be part of a NUPI, but must be part of a UPI. Consider changing to a NUPI, and adding a USI to enforce uniqueness instead.

Partition Elimination and Full Table Scans

If a SELECT request does not specify the values for all the primary index columns, an all-AMP, full-table scan is required for a table with an NPPI when there is no usable alternative index. However, with a PPI, if conditions are specified on the partitioning columns, partition elimination might reduce what would otherwise be an all-AMP, full-table scan to an all-AMP scan of only the partitions that are not eliminated. The extent of partition elimination depends on the

INDEXES

partitioning expressions, the conditions specified in the query, and the ability of the Optimizer to recognize such opportunities.

Accessing via the Primary Index in a PPI Table

If a SELECT request specifies values for all the primary index columns, the AMP that contains those rows can be determined, and only one AMP needs to be accessed. If the query conditions are not specified on the partitioning columns, then each partition can be probed to find the rows based on the hash value, assuming there is no usable alternative index. If conditions are also specified on the partitioning columns, then partition elimination might further reduce the number of partitions to be probed on that AMP.

Accessing via the Primary Index on PPI Table Workaround

With a well-constructed PPI and proper coding, access will be a one AMP and a one I/O operation. The worst case scenario with a PPI table is when a query utilizes the PI column when it is not part of the partitioning column set. In this situation, you will see an all partition scan on a single AMP in order to find the appropriate PI value. In addition, the number of disk reads could increase to equal the number of partitions on the PPI table. Even though this is a fast operation, a table with thousands of partitions could prove to be a problem for applications that require true PI performance.

One solution is to define a unique secondary index (USI) on the same column(s) as the primary index.

This approach is not as fast as accessing the non-Partitioned Primary Index column, since a USI access is always a two AMP and two I/O operation. However, a USI is independent of the number of partitions in the table and should provide good performance for applications. The second option is to ensure that users include the PI and PPI columns in their queries.

Partitioning with CASE_N

Building a partitioning expression on CASE_N or other functions and expressions is a reasonable thing to do only if the following items are *all* true:
- The partitioning expression defines a mapping between conditions and INTEGER numbers.
- The partitioning expression is not based on a DATE column.
- Your query workloads against the table use equality conditions on the partitioning columns to specify a single partition.
- The default Optimizer assumption of 9.2 quintillion partitions provides for good query plans. *Note that this does not apply to CASE_N unless the function is embedded within a larger partitioning expression.*
- You have no need to alter the partitioning of the table.
- You get the plans and data maintenance you need.

The following is an example of CASE_N partitioning.

```
CREATE TABLE Order_Table ...
PRIMARY INDEX (customer_number)
PARTITION BY CASE_N (Order_Total < 1000,      -- 1st partition
                     Order_Total < 10000,     -- 2nd partition
                     Order_Total < 100000);   -- 3rd partition
```

Figure 5.4

INDEXES

RANGE_N Partitioning

The RANGE_N function is provided to simplify the specification of common partitioning expressions where each partition contains a range of data, and is especially useful when the column contains a date. The following is an example.

```
CREATE TABLE Order_Table ...
PRIMARY INDEX (Customer_Number)
PARTITION BY RANGE_N
(Order_Date BETWEEN DATE '2001-01-01'
     AND DATE '2011-12-31'  -- 132 partitions
                EACH INTERVAL '1' MONTH);   -- defined
```

Figure 5.5

PPI with Multiple Ranges Defined

You can specify multiple ranges for a partitioning expression. The following is an example.

```
CREATE TABLE ...
PRIMARY INDEX (x)
PARTITION BY RANGE_N
( y BETWEEN 1 AND 100, 101 AND 300, 301 AND 500);
```

Figure 5.6

MLPPI

Multilevel partitioning allows each partition at a given level to be further partitioned into sub-partitions. Each partition for a level is sub-partitioned the same per a partitioning expression defined for the next lower level. The system hash orders the rows within the lowest partition levels. A multi-level PPI (MLPPI) undertakes efficient searches by using partition elimination at the various levels or combinations of levels.

The next figure is an example of creating a table with three levels of partitioning out of the maximum of 62.

```
CREATE TABLE part_x
(c1 BYTEINT
,c2 BYTEINT
,c3 BYTEINT
,c4 BYTEINT)
PRIMARY INDEX (c1, c2, c3)
PARTITION BY (RANGE_N(c1 BETWEEN 1 AND 2 EACH 1)
          ,RANGE_N(c2 BETWEEN 1 AND 2 EACH 1)
          ,RANGE_N(c3 BETWEEN 1 AND 2 EACH 1));
```

Figure 5.7

The first partitioning expression (c1) is the highest level partitioning. Within each of those partitions, the second partitioning expression (c2) defines how each of the c1 partitions is sub-partitioned. Within each of those c2 partitions, the third-level partitioning expression (c3) defines how each of the c2 partitions is sub-partitioned. Within each of these lowest level (c3) partitions, rows are ordered by the row hash value of their primary index and their assigned uniqueness value.

INDEXES

MLPPI Examples

The next example takes a previous example and modifies it in two ways. First, it adds a second level of partitioning (Order_Number), and reduces the number of Order_Date partitions so that the total number of partitions is 65,535.

```
CREATE TABLE Order_Table ...
PRIMARY INDEX (Customer_Number)
PARTITION BY
RANGE_N (Order_Date BETWEEN DATE '2010-01-01'
         AND DATE '2011-12-31'
             EACH INTERVAL '1' MONTH),
RANGE_N( Order_Number BETWEEN  122000 and 124000 EACH 1;
```

Figure 5.8

Figure 5.9 specifies 65,535 (3*5*17*257) partitions (maximum 9.2 quintillion) for a combined partitioning expression. If none of the partitioning columns are a component of the primary index, that index cannot be defined as a UPI.

Teradata 14 Solutions Development

```
CREATE TABLE markets
(productid INTEGER NOT NULL
,region BYTEINT NOT NULL
,activity_date DATE FORMAT 'yyyy-mm-dd' NOT NULL
,revenue_code BYTEINT NOT NULL
,business_sector BYTEINT NOT NULL
,note VARCHAR(256)
)
PRIMARY INDEX (productid, region)
PARTITION BY
(RANGE_N(region BETWEEN 1 AND 9 EACH 3)
,RANGE_N(business_sector BETWEEN 0 AND 49 EACH 10)
,RANGE_N(revenue_code BETWEEN 1 AND 34 EACH 2)
,RANGE_N(activity_date BETWEEN DATE '1986-01-01'
  AND DATE '2007-05-31' EACH INTERVAL '1' MONTH));
```

Figure 5.9

Rules for MLPPI

- Every RANGE_N level must have at least two partitions.
- No more than 62 levels of partitioning are allowed.
- No more than 9.2 quintillion partitions can be defined.
- BLOB, CLOB, and BIGINT are not allowed in partitioning expressions.
- CHAR values must be numeric only.
- You cannot reference the system-derived PARTITION or PARTITION#Ln columns in CREATE JOIN INDEX, CREATE HASH INDEX, or CREATE INDEX requests.
- You can reference the system-derived columns PARTITION#L1 through PARTITION#L62 at any point in a DML request where a table column can be referenced.

- You can also reference the system-derived PARTITION#L*n* columns in the DROP RANGE WHERE clause of an ALTER TABLE request.
- You can neither update these system-derived columns, nor can you assign a value or null to them with an insert operation.
- You can qualify the system-derived PARTITION#L*n* columns with a database name and table name just as you can any other table column.
- Also like the system-derived PARTITION column of single-level PPI tables, the values of the system-derived PARTITION#L*n* columns consume no space in the table. When you reference a PARTITION#L*n* column, the system extracts the internal partition number for the combined partitioning expression from the row and converts it to the external partition number for the corresponding level of the system-derived column.
- A system-derived PARTITION#L*n* column is equivalent to a value expression in which the value expression is identical to the partitioning expression at the specified level defined for the primary index.
- Like the system-derived PARTITION column for single-level PPI tables, the system derived PARTITION#L*n* columns are not included in the list of columns returned by specifying an ASTERISK character or table_name* when you select rows from a table.
- You can explicitly select a system-derived PARTITION#L*n* column from the table.
- You cannot access the system-derived PARTITION#L*n* columns through a view based on an underlying MLPPI table unless that view explicitly includes the name of the system-derived column in its definition.
- Like the system-derived PARTITION column for single-level PPI tables, the system does not return any system-derived PARTITION#L*n* columns in response to a HELP TABLE or HELP COLUMN request because they are derived and are not stored in the dictionary as names of physical columns in the table.

- Note that if you use ALTER TABLE to change one or more of the partitioning expressions for the primary index of an MLPPI table, the values of the system-derived PARTITION#Ln columns for rows in the altered table might change.

Partition Ordering

The order of partitioning expressions can be important for multilevel partitioning. The system maps multilevel partitioning expressions into a single-level combined partitioning expression. It then maps the resulting combined partition number 1-to-1 to an internal partition number. Rows are in logical ROWID order, where a ROWID consists of an internal partition number, a row hash value, and a row uniqueness value.

Partition elimination at the lowest levels can increase overhead because of the frequent need to skip to the next internal partition to be read. This is because a partition at a lower level is split among the partitions at higher levels in the partition hierarchy. At higher levels in the partition hierarchy, there are more contiguous internal partitions to scan and skip.

Determining the Rows in each Partition

There is an internal field named "PARTITION" which will return the system partition number in which a row exists. The following example loads some rows into the Part_X table created in Figure 5.7, and then retrieves all of them along with their PARTITION number.

INDEXES

```
INSERT INTO part_x VALUES(1,1,1,5);
INSERT INTO part_x VALUES(1,1,2,5);
INSERT INTO part_x VALUES(1,2,1,5);
INSERT INTO part_x VALUES(1,2,2,5);
INSERT INTO part_x VALUES(2,1,1,5);
INSERT INTO part_x VALUES(2,1,2,5);
INSERT INTO part_x VALUES(2,2,1,5);
INSERT INTO part_x VALUES(2,2,2,5);

SELECT c1, c2, c3, c4, PARTITION
FROM part_x
ORDER BY PARTITION;

  c1      c2      c3      c4     PARTITION
 ----    ----    ----    ----    ----------
   1       1       1       5          1
   1       1       2       5          2
   1       2       1       5          3
   1       2       2       5          4
   2       1       1       5          5
   2       1       2       5          6
   2       2       1       5          7
   2       2       2       5          8
```

Figure 5.10

There are additional system-derived columns, PARTITION#L1 through PARTITION#L62 that can be used to locate the rows of a specific partition. Figure 5.11 is an example.

```
SELECT c1, c2, c3, c4, PARTITION
FROM part_x
WHERE part_x.PARTITION#L2 = 1
ORDER BY PARTITION;


  c1    c2    c3    c4    PARTITION
 ----  ----  ----  ----  -----------
   1     1     1     5         1
   1     1     2     5         2
   2     1     1     5         5
   2     1     2     5         6
```

Figure 5.11

This is the equivalent of the previous code in Figure 5.11.

```
SELECT c1, c2, c3, c4, PARTITION
FROM part_x
WHERE c2 = 1
ORDER BY PARTITION;
```

Figure 5.12

Altering PPI Tables to Add or Delete Partitions

ALTER TABLE [databasename.]tablename DROP RANGE [#Ln] BETWEEN *start_expression* AND *end_expression* EACH *range_size* ;

INDEXES

- Use this form of the ALTER statement to drop a set of ranges from the RANGE_N function on which the partitioning expression for the table is based.
- #L*n* represents a partition level number where *n* is an integer between 1 and 62, inclusive.
- The expressions *start_expression* and *end_expression* are defined using the RANGE_N function.
- Ranges must be specified in ascending order.

ALTER TABLE [databasename.]tablename ADD RANGE [#L*n*] BETWEEN *start_expression* AND *end_expression* EACH *range_size* ;

- Use this form of the ALTER statement to add a set of ranges to the RANGE_N function on which the partitioning expression for the table is based.
- #L*n* represents a partition level number where *n* is an integer between 1 and 62, inclusive.
- The expressions *start_expression* and *end_expression* are defined using the RANGE_N function.
- The expressions must not have a BLOB, CLOB, or BIGINT data type.
- The *range_size* variable must be a constant expression.
- You can also add NO RANGE OR UNKNOWN and UNKNOWN specifications to the definition for the RANGE_N function.
- You can only add ranges if the partitioning expression for the table is derived exclusively from a RANGE_N function.
- Ranges must be specified in ascending order.

NO CASE, NO RANGE, or UNKNOWN

The following is the example that appeared as Figure 5.4, which defines just three partitions. The problem is that any row with a NULL Order_Total, or Order_Total equal to or greater than 100,000 will be rejected because there isn't a partition for them.

```
CREATE TABLE Order_Table ...
PRIMARY INDEX (customer_number)
PARTITION BY CASE_N (Order_Total < 1000,     -- 1st partition
                     Order_Total < 10000,    -- 2nd partition
                     Order_Total < 100000);  -- 3rd partition
```

Figure 5.13

The system provides two additional tests named NO CASE and UNKNOWN. The NO CASE partition will receive any row with an Order_Total equal to or greater than 100,000, and UNKNOWN will receive any rows having a NULL Order_Total since you can't say that NULL is less than 1,000.

Here's an example:

```
CREATE TABLE Order_Table ...
PRIMARY INDEX (customer_number)
PARTITION BY CASE_N (Order_Total < 1000,     -- 1st partition
                     Order_Total < 10000,    -- 2nd partition
                     Order_Total < 100000,   -- 3rd partition
                     NO CASE,                -- => 100000
                     UNKNOWN);               -- NULL
```

Figure 5.14

INDEXES

In the next example, NO CASE and UNKNOWN have been combined into a single partition.

```
CREATE TABLE Order_Table ...
PRIMARY INDEX (customer_number)
PARTITION BY CASE_N (Order_Total < 1000,    -- 1st partition
              Order_Total < 10000,  -- 2nd partition
              Order_Total < 100000, -- 3rd partition
              NO CASE OR
              UNKNOWN);        -- => 100000 & NULL
```

Figure 5.15

There are comparable tests for RANGE_N partitions, NO RANGE and UNKNOWN. The following example takes the table from Figure 5.4 and modifies it to capture (rather than reject) rows having partition values less than 1 or greater than 2. By declaring a partitioning column NOT NULL, the UNKNOWN test can be eliminated.

```
CREATE TABLE part_x
(c1 BYTEINT NOT NULL
,c2 BYTEINT NOT NULL
,c3 BYTEINT
,c4 BYTEINT NOT NULL)
PRIMARY INDEX (c1, c2, c3)
PARTITION BY (RANGE_N(c1 BETWEEN 1 AND 2 EACH 1, NO RANGE)
       ,RANGE_N(c2 BETWEEN 1 AND 2 EACH 1, NO RANGE)
       ,RANGE_N(c3 BETWEEN 1 AND 2 EACH 1
          NO RANGE, UNKNOWN));
```

Figure 5.16

Join Considerations and PPI

Joins can be different for PPI and NPPI tables that are otherwise equivalent, but the effect of the different join strategies that arise cannot be predicted easily in many cases.

The join plan the Optimizer pursues depends on the picture it has of the data demographics based on collected statistics, random-AMP samples, and derived statistics.

The usual recommendation applies here: check EXPLAIN reports to determine the best way to design your indexes to achieve the optimal join geography.

The following design considerations are important for this PPI performance characteristic:

- Primary index-to-primary index joins are more likely to generate different join plans than other PPI-NPPI join comparisons.
- To minimize the potential for performance issues in making primary index-to-primary index joins, consider the following guidelines:
- Partition the two tables identically if possible.
- A coarser granularity of the PPI partitions is likely to be superior to a finer partition granularity.
- Examine your EXPLAIN reports to determine which join methods the Optimizer is selecting to join the tables.
- Rowkey PPI table joins are generally better than joins based on another family of join methods.
- Efficient partition elimination can often convert joins that would otherwise be poor performers into good performers.
- The most likely candidate for poor join performance is found when you are joining a PPI table with an NPPI table, the PPI table partitioning column set is not defined in the NPPI table,

there are no predicates on the PPI table partitioning column set, and there are many partitions defined for the PPI table.
- Specify equijoins on the primary index and partitioning column sets, if possible, in order to prejudice the Optimizer to use efficient RowKey-based joins.
- Consider including the partitioning column in the NPPI table so you can join on the partition column. This means that, depending on the situation, you might want to consider denormalizing the physical schema to enhance the performance of PPI-NPPI table joins.
- If you specify an equijoin on the primary index column set, but not on the partitioning column set, the fewer combined partitions that exist after any partition elimination, the better. Otherwise, the table might need to be spooled and sorted.
- The Optimizer can specify Sliding Window Joins when there are a small number of combined partitions.
- Use RANGE_N to define fewer partitions and specify conditions on the partitioning columns to reduce the number of combined partitions involved in the join by evoking partition elimination.
- The Optimizer does not know whether a combined partition is empty or not, so it has to assume all defined combined partitions might have rows with respect to the plan it generates; however, it might choose among several such plans based on the estimated number of populated combined partitions.
- Dynamic Partition Elimination for a Product Join improves performance when a PPI table and another table are equi-joined on the partitioning column of the PPI table.
- Remember to collect statistics on all of the following:
    o The primary indexes of both tables.
    o The partitioning column of the PPI table.
    o The column in the NPPI table that is equated to the partitioning column of the PPI table.
    o The system-derived PARTITION column of the PPI table.

PPI Advantages

- Partition elimination enables large performance gains to be realizable, and these are visible to end users. For this particular optimization, more populated partitions are generally better than fewer populated partitions.
- Batch inserts and updates can run faster if the partitioning schema matches the data arrival pattern. This optimization is visible only to the DBA and operations staff.
- The largest performance improvements occur when there are no secondary indexes.
- Teradata Parallel Data Pump inserts and updates can benefit from more FSG cache hits because of the increased locality of reference when a target table is partitioned on transaction date. In this case, a finer partition granularity is generally better than a coarser partition granularity.
- Inserts into empty partitions are not journaled. This optimization is only invoked if the table has no referential integrity constraints.
- Delete operations can be nearly instantaneous when the partitioning column set matches the retention policy, there is no secondary index defined on the PPI column set, and the delete is the last statement in the transaction.
- You can delete all of the rows in a partition if you want to do so. In this case, there is no journaling of rows if no secondary index is defined on the PPI column set.
- These properties might permit you to drop a secondary index or join index on the partitioning column set.

PPI Limitations

- PPI table rows are each 2 bytes wider than the equivalent NPPI table row. The extra 2 bytes are used to store the partition number for the row.
- You cannot define the primary index of a PPI to be unique unless the entire partitioning column set is part of the primary index definition. You *can* define a USI on the primary index columns to enforce uniqueness if the complete partitioning column set is not a component of the primary index definition; however, that adds different performance issues to the equation.
- Primary index-based row access can be degraded if the partitioning column set is not a component of the primary index.
- If you can define a secondary index on the primary index column set, then performance is independent of the number of partitions.
- If you cannot, or have not, defined a secondary index on the primary index, then having fewer partitions is better than having more partitions, whether achieved by means of the table definition itself or by partition elimination during query processing.
- Joins of PPI tables to NPPI tables with the same primary index can be degraded. To combat this, observe the following guidelines:
  - Identically partition all tables to be joined with the same primary index when possible and then join them on the partitioning columns.
  - Fewer partitions, whether achieved by means of the table definition itself or by partition elimination, are often better than more partitions for the NPPI-to-PPI join scenario.

- You *cannot* use sampling to collect COLUMN statistics for the partitioning columns of PPI tables and you *should not* use sampling to collect INDEX statistics for those columns. Instead, collect statistics on the system-derived PARTITION or PARTITION#L*n* columns.

No Primary Index (NoPI) tables

Teradata now allows you to create tables without a Primary Index. These tables are called NoPI tables. When loading data into a NoPI table via TPump Array INSERT or a FastLoad, you can gain a performance advantage. This boost in performance comes from the fact that rows can be stored on any AMP allowing many rows to be packed into a single AMP step during TPump Array INSERT operations. This reduces the I/O and CPU burden. Additionally, since NoPI tables have no row-ordering constraints, rows can always be added to the end of a NoPI table by the system.

While working with a NoPI table, you are able to:

- Use INSERT/SELECT, MERGE, UPDATE/FROM SQL statements to migrate it's rows into a PI table
- Avoid full-table scans during access or delete steps by building secondary indexes
- Manipulate the rows within the NoPI table using most standard DML statements.

Things you should keep in mind while using NoPI tables:

- Creating secondary indexes on the NoPI table can reduce load times.
- You cannot use UPDATE or UPSERT to modify the data within the NoPI table.
- All access to the data is via a full-table scan if there are no secondary indexes created.

Column-Partitioned Tables

A column-partitioned table is a NoPI table where one or more columns are stored in separate partitions. Column-Partitioned tables are primarily used for data mining or analytics. Partitions are loaded via an INSERT...SELECT statement.

Things you should keep in mind while using Column-Partitioned tables:
- Permanent journals are not allowed on tables with column-partitioning.
- Column-Partitioned tables are not intended for OLTP-type workloads.

Column Partitioning and Query Performance

Column-Partitioned tables can boost performance by:
- Giving efficient access to selected data
- Unneeded columns are excluded by the optimizer

Horizontal Partitioning

By its very design, the Teradata system partitions the rows of all tables horizontally across all of the AMPs based upon the hash code of the Primary Index.

Horizontal partitioning of a very large table can be done by breaking the large table into smaller subsets. As an example, instead of a single Sales table, consider separate tables for each month.

Note: This could also be accomplished through the use of PPIs.

Creating a Partitioned Primary Index is the preferred method for horizontal partitioning. Horizontal partitioning is done at the row level.

Vertical Partitioning

When Teradata partitions a table based on rows, it is often called Horizontal Partitioning. When a table is partitioned by columns, it is called Vertical Partitioning. It allows for efficient querying of tables with large numbers of columns. Vertical partitioning can be done in several different ways:

- Physical partitioning where a table is physically split into multiple tables that contain either frequently access columns or infrequently accessed columns. This situation requires a referential integrity constraint between the two resulting tables.
- Define column partitioning while creating the table. This is used with Teradata Columnar tables. It allows the Optimizer to eliminate certain columns while processing a query.
- Defining a single-table join index or hash index on a table. An example would be a large table with 1,250 columns. Queries frequently request data from only 35 of the columns. A single-table join index or hash index could be created on just those 35 columns. This would significantly improve any queries that requested any or all of those 35 columns because the index covers the query and there is no need to scan the full table and the remaining 1,215 columns.

Join Indexes

Basic types of Join Indexes

Basically a Join Index is a persistent, materialized view. It may be based on one or more tables or be defined with pre-aggregated information. In addition, a Join Index can cover a query by containing the requested base table(s) columns. Join Indexes also have the ability to do a partial cover of a query. This means that information can be obtained from a combination of the Join Index and base table in order to satisfy the query.

There are several types of Join Indexes and each have a unique role in enhancing the performance of queries without applying denormalization techniques. Because Join Indexes are only accessed by the Optimizer and not users, they can be utilized to create persistent pre-join and summary tables while maintaining the ability to support a wide range of decision support and ad hoc queries. These denormalization techniques provide flexibility in the database without affecting the logical and physical normalization models.

The following are the basic types of Join Indexes:

- Single-Table Join Indexes
- Multi-Table Join Indexes
- Aggregate Join Indexes

The following figure illustrates these indexes.

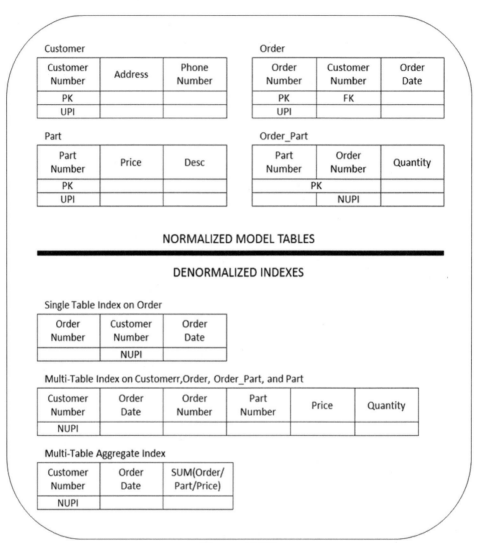

Figure 5.17

Note: An STJI may have a Primary Index different than the base table.

When to use a Join Index

Join Indexes are not suited for all applications and situations. The usefulness of a Join Index, like that of any other index, depends on the type of work it is designed to perform. The recommendation is to always prototype a Join Index in order to evaluate the benefits to the applications, along with the support required, before adding it to your production environment. In some cases, the overhead to maintain a Join Index can outweigh the benefit.

The following outlines where a Join Index could provide performance benefits:

- Frequent joins of large tables that result in a significant number of the rows being joined.
- Joins of tables with a high degree of frequency in which the same columns are repeatedly requested.
- Vertical partitioning where only a subset of data in a base table is frequently joined resulting in a redistribution of rows.
- The overhead in time and storage capacity to maintain and create a Join Index does not outweigh its retrieval benefits.

Join Index Considerations

When deciding on a Join Index strategy, the following should be considered before implementing:

- BLOB or CLOB data types are not allowed in the definition of a Join Index

- When defining a Join Index with an outer join, all columns of the outer table must be referenced in the select list of the Join Index. If they are not referenced, the system will return an error.

- Perm Space — a Join Index is a table in Teradata and uses Perm space in order to materialize the result set.

- Fallback Protection — Join Indexes can be configured with Fallback.

- MultiLoad, FastLoad, and the Teradata Parallel Transporter (TPT) LOAD and UPDATE operators cannot be used to load data when base tables have a Join Index defined. The Join Index must be dropped and recreated after the table has been loaded. However, TPump and the TPT STREAM operator support Join Indexes because they are row based update utilities.

- The loading of rows using Teradata Parallel Data Load array INSERTs into a column-partitioned or NoPI table with a Join Index defined on it can suffer.

- Archiving is permitted on a base table or database that has a Join Index defined. However, a restore will not automatically rebuild the Join Index. Instead, the Join Index is marked as invalid and will have to be dropped and recreated manually.

- Permanent journal to recover a base table with a Join Index defined is permitted. Keep in mind that the Join Index is not automatically rebuilt during the recovery process. Instead, the Join Index is marked as invalid and the Join Index must be dropped and recreated manually.

- Statistics – It is recommended that statistics should be collected on the primary index and secondary indexes of the Join Index. This will give the Optimizer the ability to choose the best path to complete the query. If the Join Index contains a UDT column, statistics cannot be collected on that column.

INDEXES

Lastly, when collecting statistics on a Join Index, you should always consider using the SAMPLE options.

Join Indexes versus Other Options

Remember, the goal is to leave the base tables fully normalized and to create other solutions. The following charts compare Join Indexes against views, summary tables, and temporary tables.

Join Indexes versus Views

Join Index	View
Rows are physically stored on the disks.	Rows are compiled each time the view is referenced.
Ability to have a Primary Index.	Cannot have a Primary Index.
Main function is to increase access speed to data.	Main function is to manipulate how data is seen in reports, and for security.
Rows are not accessible to users.	Rows are accessible to users with the proper rights.

Figure 5.18

Join Indexes versus Summary Tables

Join Index	Summary Tables
Rows are physically stored on the disks.	Rows are physically stored on the disks.
Ability to have a Primary Index.	Ability to have Primary Index.
Uses up Perm space.	Uses up Perm Space
Main function is to increase access speed to data – maintained by RDBMS.	Main function is to increase access speed to data – users have to maintain.
Rows are not accessible to users	Rows are accessible to users with the proper rights.

Figure 5.19

Join Indexes versus Temporary Tables

Join Index	Temporary Tables
Rows are physically stored on the disks.	Rows are in Spool or Temp space.
Ability to have a Primary Index.	Ability to have Primary Index.
Uses up Perm space.	Does not use Perm Space.
Main function is to increase access speed to data.	Main function is to allow for a quick and disposable look at the data.
Rows are not accessible to users	Rows are accessible to users with the proper rights.

Figure 5.20

Single-Table Join Index

Single-Table Join Indexes are one of the most useful constructs for tactical queries. The real benefit is that you are allowed to partition all or a subset of a very large base table as a "join index" on a different primary index than that used by the original base table in order to hash its rows to the same AMPs as another very large base table that it is frequently joined to.

If a variable small subset of columns and rows are to be accessed on a regular basis, you can create a Column-Partitioned Join Index. While creating a CPJI, it cannot:

- Have a primary index
- Compute aggregates
- Have value-ordering
- Be row-compressed

The following figure shows a Single-Table Join Index (STJI) built on the Order table, but with its Primary Index based on the Customer_Number column.

INDEXES

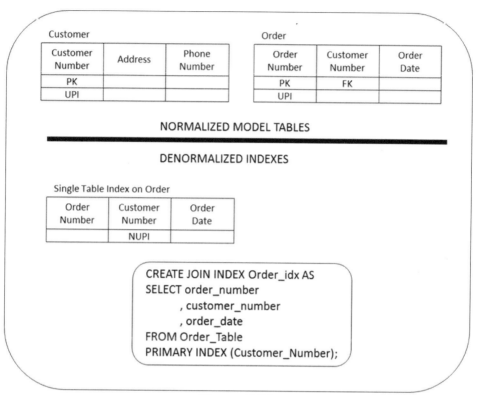

Figure 5.21

If a user queries the Order table with an equality condition on Order_Number, the system can use the base table's UPI for access. If the user queries the Order table with an equality condition on Customer_Number, the system can use the NUPI of the index for access. If the user does a join between the Customer and Order tables, the rows of the index are already on the same AMP as the Customer rows, so now the system can do a PI to PI join.

Simple Join Index

A Simple, or Multi-Table Join Index is defined as creating a Join Index that involves more than one table, generally for joins of known queries. The essence behind a multi-table Join Index is that Teradata stores an answer set of an often-used query on disk. For example, Join Indexes for an outer join have the ability to preserve the unmatched rows resulting from the join. This is beneficial because this allows the Join Index to optimize more queries that have few join conditions. When all columns required by a query are available via a Join Index, this is an example of a Covered Query.

The following diagram shows a three-table Join Index.

INDEXES

Customer

Customer Number	Address	Phone Number
PK		
UPI		

Order

Order Number	Customer Number	Order Date
PK	FK	
UPI		

Part

Part Number	Price	Desc
PK		
UPI		

Order_Part

Part Number	Order Number	Quantity
PK		
	NUPI	

NORMALIZED MODEL TABLES

DENORMALIZED INDEXES

Multi-Table Index on Order, Order_Part, and Part

Customer Number	Order Date	Order Number	Part Number	Price	Quantity
NUPI					

```
CREATE JOIN INDEX  Order_Part_idx AS
SELECT  Customer_Number
      , Order_Date
      , Order_Number
      , Part_Number
      , Price
      , Quantity
FROM Order JOIN Order_Part
ON Order.Order_Number = Order_Part.Order_Number
JOIN Part
ON Order_Part.Part_Number = Part.Part_Number
Primary Index (Customer_Number);
```

Figure 5.22

Aggregate Join Index

If an application consistently accesses the same table or multi-table join with data aggregation, then an aggregate Join Index can offer some performance benefits. This is achieved by allowing you to pre-aggregate values once and then use them one or more times.

Keep in mind the following when implementing an Aggregate Join Index:

- Only sums and counts may be used in an Aggregate Join Index.
- All aggregation columns defined in the select list must include an "as" alias.
- The DISTINCT command is not permitted.
- COUNT and SUM columns should be defined as type FLOAT to avoid overflow.
- An AGI cannot be column-partitioned

The next diagram shows creating an aggregate index.

INDEXES

Customer

Customer Number	Address	Phone Number
PK		
UPI		

Order

Order Number	Customer Number	Order Date
PK	FK	
UPI		

Part

Part Number	Price	Desc
PK		
UPI		

Order_Part

Part Number	Order Number	Quantity
PK	PK	
	NUPI	

NORMALIZED MODEL TABLES

DENORMALIZED INDEXES

Multi-Table Aggregate Index

Customer Number	Order Date	SUM(Order/Part/Price)
NUPI		

```
CREATE JOIN INDEX Agg_Order_idx AS
SELECT  Customer_Number
, EXTRACT (MONTH FROM Order_Date AS Order_Month
, SUM( Part.Price * Order_Part.Quantity)  (DEC (6,2)) AS Order_Total
FROM Order JOIN Order_Part
ON Order.Order_Number = Order_Part.Order_Number
JOIN Part
ON Order_Part.Part_Number = Part.Part_Number
GROUP BY 1, 2
PRIMARY INDEX ( Customer_Number) ;
```

Figure 5.23

Sparse Indexes

The sparse Join Index feature is a particularly useful variation of a Join Index. A WHERE clause in the CREATE JOIN INDEX statement limits the rows from the base table that will participate in the sparse Join Index, making a smaller, often quicker to build structure. Any Join Index, whether simple or aggregate, multi-table or single-table, can be sparse.

Sparse indexes, like other index choices, should be chosen to support high frequency queries that require short response times. Typically Sparse Join Indexes provide the following benefits:

- Reduces the storage requirements for a Join Index
- Makes access faster since the size of the JI is smaller
- Use only a portion of the columns in the base table.
- Index only the values you want to index.
- Ignore some columns, e.g., nulls, to keep access smaller and faster than before.
- Avoid maintenance costs for updates

Most Sparse Join Indexes are limited by date as shown below.

```
CREATE JOIN INDEX Order_2011 AS
SELECT Order_Number
     , Customer_Number
     , Order_Date
FROM Order
WHERE EXTRACT(YEAR FROM Order_Date) = 2011
PRIMARY INDEX(Customer_Number) ;
```

Figure 5.24

Sparse indexes, such as the above example, have good performance when it comes to join performance, along with updating the base

INDEXES

table, because of the smaller subset of data being utilized for the sparse index, as illustrated below.

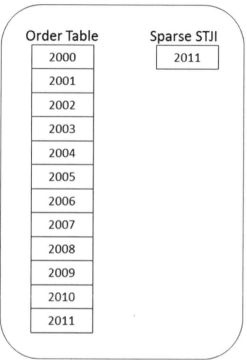

Figure 5.25

Global Join Index

Suppose there is a large table that needs to be joined frequently with another table on a column that is not the distributing column of the table. You can define a join index that redistributes the base table by the join column. However, because of the large number of rows and columns that need to be projected into the join index, the extra disk storage required does not allow the creation of such a join index.

You can define a join index in such a way that its partial coverage of a query can be extended further by joining with a parent base table to pick up any columns requested by the query but not referenced in the join index definition.

A Global Index is basically a Join Index that contains a direct link to the base table rows. When you include the Row ID in a Join Index, the Row ID (Part # + Row Hash + Uniqueness Value) is stored. Global Indexes provide the following:

- Improved performance for certain classes of queries.
- Can provide reduced duplication of all the columns required to cover the queries resulting in better performance.
- Improved scalability for certain classes of queries

However, Global Indexes do have limitations which include:

- Aggregate JI does not support the partial-covering capability.
- Global Index is not used for correlated sub-queries.
- Global Index is not supported with FastLoad or MultiLoad.

Partial-Covering Global Join Indexes can provide:

- Can be a single-table or a set of joined tables that has an access path to a base table.
- Each Index row points back to the real base row in the real base table.
- Will have rows hashed to a different AMP than the rows of the base table.
- Is very similar to a hashed NUSI but most likely won't access all the AMPs.
- Is also similar to a hashed USI, but most likely will be more than a 2-AMP operation.

ODS (Operational Data Store) or tactical queries that involve an equality condition on a fairly unique column can use a global index which will change:

- Table-level locks to row hash locks
- All-AMP steps to group-AMP steps

Global Join Index – Multi-Table Join Back

Join back simply means that the ROWID is carried as part of the Join Index. This permits the index to "join back" to the base row, much like a NUSI does. The following illustrates this feature.

```
CREATE JOIN INDEX CustOrdGlobal_IDX AS
SELECT c.customer_number
, c.ROWID AS Cust_Rowid
, c.Address
, c.Phone
, o.Order_Number
, o.ROWID AS Order_Rowid
, o.Order_Date
FROM Customer AS c JOIN Order AS o
ON c.Customer_Number = o.Customer_Number
PRIMARY INDEX(c.Customer_Number) ;
```

Figure 5.26

The total number of columns that you can use in a Global Join Index is 64. If the number of columns in both tables is more than 64, the recommendation is to only include the most frequently referenced columns from each table. Another reason to only include a subset of columns is to minimize the size of the Join Index.

In this case, the Join Index sub-table row will also include the Row ID of the base table row for the Customer table and the Row ID of the base table for the Orders table. The optimizer may choose to use the Join Index to get most of the data and join back to either the Customer or the Orders table to get additional requested data.

Starting with V2R5, the optimizer can build execution plans that can join back to either table. The terminology used in EXPLAIN plans that indicate a join back is "… using a row id join …".

Global Join Index as a "Hash NUSI"

Global Join Index (GJI) on a single table is known as a Hashed NUSI. Keep in mind that typical NUSI is an all AMPs operation; however, GJI hash index only accesses the AMPs that have rows it requires based on the SQL statement. From there, the GJI index will use the Row IDs in this sub-table to access only those AMPs that have rows.

Utilizing a global index in this situation is similar to a single-table Join Indexe with one clear distinction, which is the GJI carries the ROWID back to the base table, and is used as an alternative means to get to the base table rows.

A "Hashed NUSI" global index also combines the best of a NUSI, which supports duplicate values, and a USI, which is hash-distributed on the indexed value which provides the ability to conduct group AMP processing. As discussed throughout this chapter, Global Join Indexes are transparent to the query and its use will be determined solely by the optimizer.

The true value of the GJI hashed NUSI is for situations where your result set is small and you want to avoid an all AMP operation that a NUSI always requires. This may not have a performance impact for systems that are small in size. However, for very large systems, with hundreds of AMPs, a group AMP operation that engages a small percentage of AMPs with this tactic, could increase overall throughput as well as faster query response times.

Identity Columns

To have the system automatically create a unique identifier for each row, define one numeric column as an IDENTITY column. IDENTITY columns are valuable for generating simple unique indexes and primary and surrogate keys when composite indexes or keys are not desired.

The data type for an identity column is user-defined, but must be an exact numeric type drawn from the following list:

- BIGINT
- BYTEINT
- DECIMAL(n,0)
- INTEGER
- NUMERIC(n,0)
- SMALLINT

In general, you should define the column to be either DECIMAL or NUMERIC, with the value for *n* being the largest number available for your system.

Note that the largest size identity column the system produces is that specified by a DECIMAL(18,0) or NUMERIC(18,0) specification. This is true even when the DBSControl field MaxDecimal is set to 38 (see *SQL Reference: Data Types and Literals* and *Utilities*). You can define an identity column with more than 18 digits of precision, or even as a BIGINT type, without the CREATE TABLE or ALTER TABLE statement aborting, but the values generated by the identity column feature remain limited to the DECIMAL(18,0) type and size.

Identity columns have many applications, including the automatic generation of UPIs, USIs, and PKs. Values generated for GENERATED ALWAYS AS IDENTITY columns are always unique, but those generated for GENERATED BY DEFAULT AS IDENTITY are only unique if you also specify a UNIQUE constraint on the column.

Do *not* attempt to update GENERATE ALWAYS identity column values under any circumstances. This operation is not permitted and the system returns an error if you attempt to perform it.

The general syntax for an IDENTITY column definition is shown below:

GENERATED { ALWAYS | BY DEFAULT } AS IDENTITY
[(counting-definitions)]

GENERATED ALWAYS	<ul><li>Columns cannot be updated.</li><li>Column values that also specify NO CYCLE are guaranteed to be unique.</li><li>Cannot be null.</li><li>If you load the same row twice into an identity column table, it is not rejected as a duplicate because it is made unique as soon as an identity column value is generated for it. This means that some preprocessing must still be performed on rows to be loaded into identity column tables if real world uniqueness is a concern.</li></ul>
GENERATED BY DEFAULT	<ul><li>The system generates a value (explicitly or implicitly) by an INSERT statement.</li><li>Columns can be updated.</li><li>Column values are not guaranteed to be unique.</li><li>Cannot be null.</li><li>To guarantee uniqueness you must:</li></ul>

INDEXES

	<ul><li>Specify NO CYCLE.</li><li>Any user specified values can be inside or outside the range of any system-generated values.</li><li>You must enforce the uniqueness of the user-specified values yourself.</li></ul>

Figure 5.27

The counting definitions are as follows:

START WITH <v1>	Unless specified otherwise, counting starts at 1.
INCREMENT BY <v2>	Unless specified otherwise, the system increments by +1. Can decrement if a negative value is specified.
MINVALUE <v3> NO MINVALUE	Can specify a limit for decrementing values.
MAXVALUE <v4> NO MAXVALUE	Can specify a limit for incrementing values.
[NO] CYCLE	Can specify whether deleted values can be reused.

Figure 5.28

An example:

```
CREATE MULTISET TABLE test01 (
a1 INTEGER GENERATED BY DEFAULT AS IDENTITY
   (START WITH 1
    INCREMENT BY 20
    MAXVALUE 1000
   ),
a2 INTEGER);
```

Figure 5.29

You cannot add an identity column to an existing table, nor can you add the identity column attribute to an existing column.

You can drop an identity column from an existing table, but you cannot drop just the identity column attribute and retain the column.

Note: Column compression is not supported for Identity columns.

Chapter 5: Practice Questions

1. How many NUSI equality conditions must be ANDed together for the Parser to consider NUSI Bitmapping?
    a. Two
    b. Three
    c. Four

2. Which of the following is true for the sort key for a Value Ordered NUSI?
    a. Single column, any data type
    b. Single column, numeric data type
    c. Multiple columns, any data type
    d. Multiple columns, numeric data type

3. What is the maximum number of non-primary indexes you can define on a base or join index table?
    a. 12
    b. 16
    c. 32
    d. 48
    e. 64

4. A table with a trigger _____
    a. can have a Join Index but not a Hash Index.
    b. can have a Hash Index but not a Join Index.
    c. cannot have either.
    d. can have both.

5. Which of the following statement is true?
    a. A hash index may be valued ordered.
    b. A hash index may not be value ordered.

Teradata 14 Solutions Development

6. Which statement is true about a queue table?
   a. It may not have a PPI.
   b. It may have a single-level PPI but not a multi-level PPI.
   c. It may have either a single-level or multi-level PPI.

7. Which is truer for RANGE_N partitioning?
   a. It's better with dates.
   b. It's better with integer numbers.

8. Batch inserts and updates to a PPI table can run faster if the data arrival pattern _____.
   a. matches the partitioning schema
   b. matches the QITS column
   c. is sorted on non-partitioning columns

9. An example of horizontal partitioning is:
   a. PPI
   b. NUSI Bit Mapping
   c. Value Ordered NUSI

10. Which of the following aggregation operators can appear in an Aggregate Join Index?
    a. AVG
    b. COUNT
    c. MAX
    d. MIN
    e. SUM

11. The total number of columns you can use in a Global Join Index is:
    a. 16
    b. 32
    c. 64
    d. 128
    e. 256
    f. 512

12. Which of the following data types cannot be used for Identity Columns?
    a. BIGINT
    b. BYTEINT
    c. DECIMAL
    d. FLOAT
    e. INTEGER
    f. NUMERIC
    g. SMALLINT

13. Which of the following statements is true for an identity column set table?
    a. You can load the same row twice.
    b. You cannot load the same row twice.

14. Choose the correct statement about identity columns.
    a. They can be added to existing tables.
    b. They can be compressed.
    c. They can be any numeric data type.
    d. All of the above.
    e. None of the above.

Chapter Notes

Utilize this space for notes, key points to remember, diagrams, areas of further study, etc.

Chapter 6 - Joins and Explain

Certification Objectives

- ✓ Given a scenario including table definitions, a query, and an EXPLAIN, identify opportunities for optimization.
- ✓ Given a join plan, describe the operation of a join.
- ✓ Describe the operations occurring when key phrases are seen in an EXPLAIN.

Before You Begin

You should be familiar with the following terms and concepts.

Terms	Key Concepts
Joining tables	SQL syntax
Join plans	What are they and why would the Parser choose one over another.
EXPLAIN	Terms, meanings, and usefulness.

Joins

In this chapter we will use the term 'relation' as being some set of data, involved in a join, that is either derived (i.e. spool space) or pre-defined (permanent space).

Also, this chapter will illustrate how the complete cost for processing a join is based upon the cost of its preparation steps as well as the cost for doing the join. The context of this discussion focuses mainly on the join itself."

Changing Data Types to Enhance Performance

If possible, design your tables and queries so that the joined fields are from the same domain and have identical data type. If numeric, make sure they are the same size. If the joined fields are of different data types (i.e. different sizes or numeric values), changing the data type of one of the tables will improve join performance by avoiding the costly data type conversion.

In such cases, if the same data types are specified on the joined fields and they are the primary index, then the Optimizer may process the join without the need for join preparation.

Joins can be performed on either equality or inequality comparison, but are usually used for equal comparisons. Like in a single table SELECT, each table is listed following the FROM clause.

The following diagram shows the simplified join syntax.

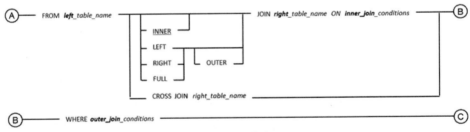

Figure 6.1

JOINS AND EXPLAIN

The impact on Join Strategies with the Optimizer

The Optimizer will analyze the user's query and review the join types within the query. Upon conclusion of the review, the optimizer will choose the best join plan (by selecting a join strategy) for the query and execute the request.

For the sake of review, let's briefly discuss the different types of joins that can be written in SQL:

- **Inner Join:** Returns matching rows from both tables. No unmatched rows are returned.
- **Left Outer:** Returns the matched rows from both tables. Also returns any unmatched rows from table on the left side of the join.
- **Right Outer:** Returns the matched rows from both tables. Also returns any unmatched rows from table on the right side of the join.
- **Full Outer:** Returns both the matched and unmatched rows from both tables (Inner, Left, and Right).
- **Self Join:** Compares columns inside the table against other columns inside the exact same table to return matching rows.
- **Cross Join:** Compares each row in the first table to each row of the second table, resulting in the return of all rows in the first table multiplied by the number of rows in the second table.

Join Strategies

The following is a list of join strategies which the optimizer will choose from:

- Merge Join
- Nested Join
- Hash Join
- Exclusion Join
- Inclusion Join
- Product Join (Cartesian Join)

Join Types

Inner Joins

Inner joins only return the qualifying rows within each relation from the left table and right table that match the ON join condition. Figure 6.2 illustrates this.

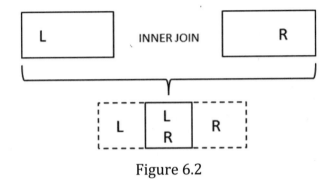

Figure 6.2

Outer Joins

Left Outer Join

In a LEFT OUTER JOIN, the rows from the left table that are *not* returned in the result of the inner join of the two tables are returned in the outer join relation resulting in the inner relation to be extended with nulls. Figure 6.3 shows this.

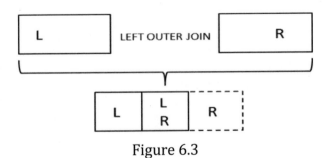

Figure 6.3

Right Outer Join

In a RIGHT OUTER JOIN, the rows from the right table that are *not* returned in the result of the inner join of the two tables are returned in the outer join relation resulting in the inner table to be extended with nulls, as shown below.

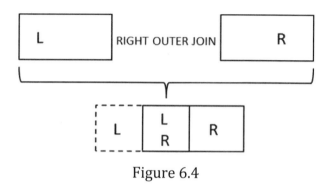

Figure 6.4

Full Outer Join

In a FULL OUTER JOIN, project rows from both tables that have *not* been returned in the result of the inner join will be returned in the outer join relation (both right and left) resulting in nulls, as illustrated below.

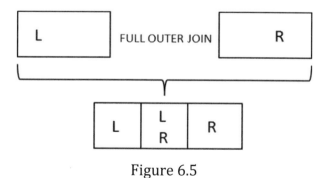

Figure 6.5

Self Joins

A self-join joins a table to itself. This type of join occurs when a particular column value resembles/repeats in another column of a same table. For example, attempting to find employees who are managers.

Cross Joins

A CROSS JOIN is a Product Join. This is where <u>Every</u> row of the left table is joined to <u>every</u> row of the right table.

Join Strategies

Merge Joins

The Merge Join retrieves rows and sorts the rows into join column row hash sequence, then joins those rows that have matching join column row hash values.

The Merge Join projects or retrieves column values for rows of two relations. Unlike many of the other strategies, these also require sorting both tables (relations) of the join on the hash of the join columns. Like any other operation, the data involved (in this case, to compare values for a join) must be AMP local. In a Merge Join, the columns on which tables are matched are also the columns on which both tables, or redistributed spools of tables, are ordered.

Join Strategies: Merge Strategy #1

Before two rows (or relation) can be joined, they must be on the same AMP. If the join columns are the Primary Indexes of the two tables, matching rows are already on common AMPs. No redistribution is

JOINS AND EXPLAIN

required. The system can proceed directly to the join without preparation. Here's an example.

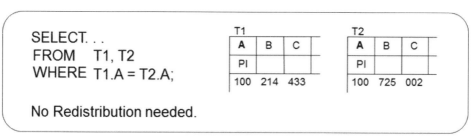

Figure 6.6

Join Strategies: Merge Strategy #2

Before two rows (or relation) can be joined, they must be on the same AMP. In the following diagram, the Primary Index of T3 is being joined to a non-Primary Index column. In this case, the system can hash redistribute copies of the T4 rows. Once that step is finished, the system can proceed to the join.

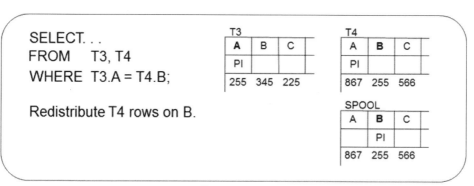

Figure 6.7

Join Strategies: Merge Strategy #3

Before two rows can be joined, they must be on the same AMP.

In this next example, the join columns are not the Primary Index of either table (or relation). What the system can do in this case is to hash redistribute copies of both tables based on the row hash of the join column values.

Once the two tables have been redistributed, the system can proceed to the join:

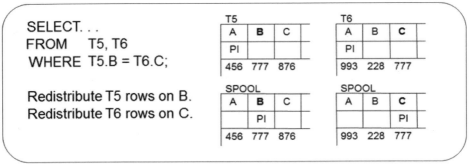

Figure 6.8

Join Strategies: Merge Strategy #4

Before two rows can be joined, they must be on the same AMP. A Rowkey join includes the row's partition number as well as its Row Hash.

Joining two relations where one is value partitioned (using PPI or MLPPI) and the other is hash partitioned may result in the database:

1. Optionally - redistribute on the PI of hash partitioned relation into spool
2. Required - sort on row hash within partition value based on the partition expression of PPI relation (the row-key)

3. Perform a merge join within matching partitions of the two relations.

Nested Joins

This is a special join case. This is the only join that doesn't always use all of the AMPs. It is the most efficient in terms of system resources. It is the best choice for OLTP applications. To choose a Nested Join, the Optimizer must have:

- An equality value for a unique index (UPI or USI) on Table1.
- An equijoin on a column of that single row to any index on Table2.
- The system retrieves the single row from Table1.
- It hashes the join column value to access matching Table2 row(s).

The following diagram shows the various combinations of a nested join.

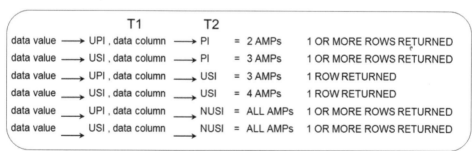

Figure 6.9

Hash Joins

Hash Join is applicable when the entire small table fits into available memory. The system reads rows from the small table directly into a memory-resident hash table.

The process then reads rows from the large table and uses them to individually probe the hash table for a match. A result row is returned for each hash match that satisfies all the join conditions.

Inclusion and Exclusion Join

Exclusion joins are performed (typically) as a variation of "merge" or "product" join, (e.g. referencing IN or NOT IN). When referencing NOT IN (Exclusion form), they are only performed if the matching column sets are defined as NOT NULL. For the IN reference (Inclusion form) NULL definitions are irrelevant.

Product Joins

This is the most general form of a join. Any join type can be performed as a Product Join. In general:

1. Identifies the small relation and duplicates it on each AMP (no sorting is performed)
2. Compare each and every set of join columns from one relation to each and every set of join columns of the other relation
3. Project or retrieve column values for each set of qualifying rows

JOINS AND EXPLAIN

It is called a Product Join because:

Total Compares = # Qualified Table1 Rows * # Qualified Table2 Rows

Although the join step itself can be very expensive, the preparation step may be cheap enough to make this strategy better performing overall.

Note: Product joins are also called Unrestricted or Restricted Cartesian Product Joins.

EXPLAIN Terminology

To review the query plan of any valid Teradata SQL statement, you would use the EXPLAIN facility. However, the EXPLAIN modifier (or request) *cannot* be utilized with the following;

- A USING request modifier (see *SQL Reference: Data Manipulation Statements*).
- Individual functions, or stored procedures.

Most EXPLAIN text is easy to understand. The following additional definitions may be helpful:

... (Last Use) ...
A spool file is no longer needed and will be released when this step completes.

... with no residual conditions ...
All applicable conditions have been applied to the rows.

... END TRANSACTION ...

Transaction locks are released, changes are committed, and the Transient Journal images are released.

... eliminating duplicate rows ...
(Duplicate rows only exist in spool files, not set tables.) Doing a DISTINCT operation.

... by way of the sort key in spool field1 ...
Field1 is created to allow a tag sort.

... we do an ABORT test ...
Caused by an ABORT or ROLLBACK statement.

Note: ROLLBACK is ANSI compliant and ABORT is an equivalent extension.

... by way of a traversal of index #n extracting row ids only ...
A spool file is built containing the Row IDs found in a secondary index (index #n).

... we do a BMSMS (bit map set manipulation step)
Doing a NUSI Bit Map operation.

... which is redistributed by hash code to all AMPs.
... which is duplicated on all AMPs.

Relocating data in preparation for a join.

... (one_AMP) or (group_AMPs)
indicates one AMP or a subset of AMPs will be used instead of all AMPs.

... ("NOT (table_name.column_name IS NULL)")
feature in which the optimizer realizes that the column being joined to is NOT NULL or has referential integrity.

JOINS AND EXPLAIN

... Joined using a row id join ...
Usually occurs due to applying a 'join-back' strategy from a single-table join index" (joining a relation consisting of rowids to another relation, regardless of how the rowids relation was generated.

Full Table Scan

The following Explain shows a full-table scan.

```
EXPLAIN SELECT * FROM employee_table;
```

Figure 6.10

```
  1) First, we lock a distinct CSQL_CLASS."pseudo table"
     for read on a RowHash to prevent global deadlock for
     CSQL_CLASS.employee_table.
  2) Next, we lock CSQL_CLASS.employee_table for read.
  3) We do an all-AMPs RETRIEVE step from
     CSQL_CLASS.employee_table by way of an all-rows scan
     with no residual conditions into Spool 1 (group_amps),
     which is built locally on the AMPs.  The size of Spool
     1 is estimated with low confidence to be 6 rows (546
     bytes).
     The estimated time for this step is 0.03 seconds.
  4) Finally, we send out an END TRANSACTION step to all
     AMPs involved in processing the request.
 -> The contents of Spool 1 are sent back to the user as
     the result of statement 1.  The total estimated time
     is 0.03 seconds.
```

Unique Primary Index (UPI)

The following is an Explain of a UPI retrieval.

```
EXPLAIN   SELECT * FROM employee_table WHERE employee_no =
2000000;
```

Figure 6.11

```
1) First, we do a single-AMP RETRIEVE step from
   CSQL_CLASS.EMPLOYEE_TABLE by way of the unique primary
   index "CSQL_CLASS.EMPLOYEE_TABLE.Employee_No =
   2000000" with no residual conditions.  The estimated
   time for this step is 0.01 seconds.
-> The row is sent directly back to the user as the
   result of statement 1.  The total estimated time is
   0.01 seconds.
```

Non-Unique Primary Index (NUPI)

The following shows an Explain of a NUPI retrieval.

EXPLAIN SELECT * FROM emp_job_table WHERE job_no = 30010;

Figure 6.12

```
1) First, we do a single-AMP RETRIEVE step from
   CSQL_CLASS.EMP_job_table by way of the primary index
   "CSQL_CLASS.EMP_job_table.job_no = 30010" with no
   residual conditions into Spool 1 (one-amp), which is
   built locally on that AMP.  The size of Spool 1 is
   estimated with low confidence to be 2 rows (58 bytes).
   The estimated time for this step is 0.02 seconds.
-> The contents of Spool 1 are sent back to the user as
   the result of statement 1.  The total estimated time
   is 0.02 seconds.
```

Unique Secondary Index (USI)

The following is an Explain of a USI retrieval.

EXPLAIN SELECT * FROM emp_job_table WHERE job_no = 20010 AND emp_no = 1121334;

Figure 6.13

```
1) First, we do a two-AMP RETRIEVE step from
```

JOINS AND EXPLAIN

   CSQL_CLASS.emp_job_table by way of unique index # 4
   "CSQL_CLASS.emp_job_table.job_no   =   20010,
   CSQL_CLASS.emp_job_table.emp_no = 1121334" with no
   residual conditions. The estimated time for this step
   is 0.01 seconds.
-> The row is sent directly back to the user as the
   result of statement 1. The total estimated time is
   0.01 seconds.

Non-Unique Secondary Index (NUSI)

Here's an Explain of a NUSI retrieval.

> EXPLAIN SELECT * FROM STUDENT_TABLE WHERE class_code = 'FR';

Figure 6.14

1) First, we lock a distinct CSQL_CLASS."pseudo table"
for read on a RowHash to prevent global deadlock for
CSQL_CLASS.student_table.
 2) Next, we lock CSQL_CLASS.student_table for read.
 3) We do an all-AMPs RETRIEVE step from
    CSQL_CLASS.student_table by way of index # 4
    "CSQL_CLASS.student_table.class_code = 'FR'with no
    residual conditions into Spool 1, which is built
    locally on the AMPs. The size of Spool 1 is estimated
    with low confidence to be 2 rows (182 bytes).
    The estimated time for this step is 0.03 seconds.
 4) Finally, we send out an END TRANSACTION step to all
    AMPs involved in processing the request.
-> The contents of Spool 1 are sent back to the user as
   the result of statement 1. The total estimated time
   is 0.03 seconds.

Pseudo Locks

"Pseudo Table" Locks prevent two users from getting conflicting locks with all-AMP requests. Figure 6.15 illustrates this.

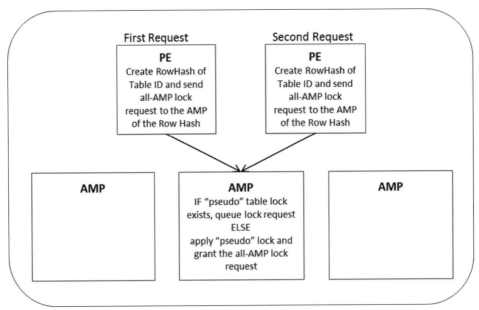

Figure 6.15

Confidence Levels

The EXPLAIN facility may express "confidence" for a retrieve from a table.

Some of the phrases used are:

... with high confidence ...
- Restricting conditions exist on index(es) or column(s) that have collected statistics.

... with low confidence ...
- Restricting conditions exist on index(es) having no statistics, but estimates can be based upon a sampling of the index(es).

– Restricting conditions exist on index(es) or column(s) that have collected statistics but are "ANDed" together with conditions on non-indexed columns.
– Restricting conditions exist on index(es) or column(s) that have collected statistics but are "ORed" together with other conditions.

. . . with no confidence . . .
– Conditions outside the above.

The following are "confidence" phrases for a join:

. . . with index join confidence . . .
– A join condition via a primary index.

. . . with high confidence . . .
– One input relation has high confidence and the other has high or index join confidence.

. . . with low confidence . . .
– One input relation has low confidence and the other has low, high, or join index confidence.

. . . with no confidence . . .
– One input relation has no confidence.
– Statistics do not exist for either join field.

Query Cost Estimates

Row estimates:
- May be estimated using random samples, statistics or indexes
- Are assigned a confidence level - high, low or none
- Affect timing estimates - more rows, more time needed

Timings:
- Used to determine the 'lowest cost' plan
- Total cost generated if all processing steps have assigned cost

Miscellaneous Notes:
- Estimates too large to display show 3 asterisks (***).
- The accuracy of the time estimate depends upon the accuracy of the row estimate.
- Low and no confidence may indicate a need to collect statistics on indexes or columns involved in restricting conditions.
- You may otherwise consider a closer examination of the conditions in the query for possible changes that may improve the confidence.
- Collecting statistics or altering the conditions has no real impact unless it influences the optimizer to pick a better plan.

Execute the following steps in Parallel

PARALLEL STEPS are AMP steps that can execute concurrently:
- They have no functional overlap and do not contend for resources.
- They improve performance.
- The Optimizer generates PARALLEL STEPS whenever possible.
- EXPLAIN text identifies Parallel Steps.

The following diagram shows an example of parallel steps.

JOINS AND EXPLAIN

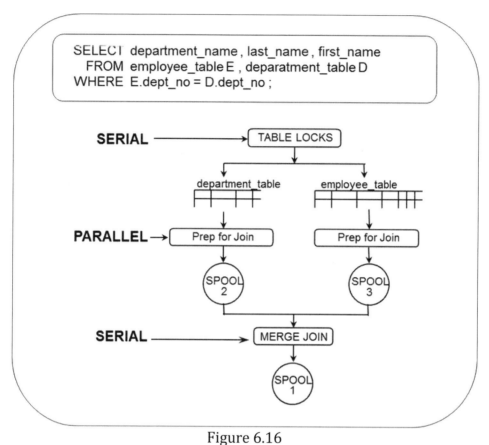

Figure 6.16

Redistributed by Hash Code

This is a join table preparation step. It means the system is moving row copies to put them on the same AMPs as the rows they are to be joined to. This is typically an example of doing a PI join to a non-PI column set.

Duplicated on All AMPs

This is another join preparation step. Each AMP sends copies of its qualifying rows and columns to all of the AMPs, which results in every AMP having a complete copy of the qualifying rows.

Join Index

If a Join Index exists, the Parser will use it if it's the least expensive solution. The following is an Explain where the Parser used the JI instead of accessing the underlying base tables.

```
SELECT o.order_date
     , COUNT (c.customer_id)
FROM customer_table c
INNER JOIN order_table o
ON c.customer_no = o.customer_no
WHERE o.order_date = '2008-08-18'
GROUP BY 1;
```

Figure 6.17

```
1) First, we lock CSQL_CLASS.customer_order_idx for read.
2) Next, we do a SUM step to aggregate from join index
   table CSQL_CLASS.customer_order_idx by way of an all-
   rows scan with a condition of
   "CSQL_CLASS.customer_order_idx.order_date = DATE '2008-
   08-18'"), and the grouping identifier in field 1.
   Aggregate Intermediate Results are computed globally,
   then placed in Spool 3. The size of Spool 3 is estimated
   with high confidence to be 1 rows.
3) We do an all-AMPs RETRIEVE step from Spool 3 (Last Use)
   by way of an all-rows scan into Spool 1, which is built
   locally on the AMPs. The size of Spool 1 is estimated
   with high confidence to be 1 row. The estimated time for
   this step is 0.17 seconds.
4) Finally, we send out an END TRANSACTION step to all AMPs
   involved in processing the request.
-> The contents of Spool 1 are sent back to the user as the
```

JOINS AND EXPLAIN

```
result of statement 1.  The total estimated time is 0.17
seconds.
```

BMSMS Bit Mapping

BMSMS = Bit Map Set Manipulation Step = NUSI Bit Mapping. This is a processing step where the system combines multiple weakly selective equality NUSIs that are ANDed together to reduce the number of I/Os to the base table.

PPI Tables and Partitions

The following are phrases associated with PPI tables and their partitions.

"*a single partition of*" or "*n partitions of*"
- Indicates that an AMP or AMPs only need to access a single partition or *n partitions of a table*
- Indicates *partition elimination occurred.*
- Partition elimination can occur for SELECTs, UPDATEs, and DELETEs.
- For a DELETE, Optimizer recognizes partitions in which all rows are deleted.
- Rows in such partitions are deleted without using the transient journal.

"*all partitions of*"
- All partitions are accessed for primary index access in processing the query. It is used with primary-indexed tables or join indexes that are row-partitioned. It is not applicable to either column-partitioned join-indexes or tables because, by definition, those objects lack a primary index.

Teradata 14 Solutions Development

"SORT to partition Spool m by rowkey"
- The spool is to be sorted by rowkey (Partition and ROWID).
- Partitioning the spool file in this way allows for a faster join with the partitioned table.

"a rowkey-based"
- The join is hash-based by partition (rowkey). In this case, there are equality constraints on both the partitioning and primary index columns.
- When this phrase is not reported, then the join is hash-based.

"enhanced by dynamic partition ..."
- Indicates a join condition where dynamic partition elimination has been used.

"of a single partition" or *"of n partitions"*
- The optimizer determined that all rows in a single partition, or *n* partitions, can be utilized or deleted in a query operation.
- In some cases, this allows for faster deletion of the entire partition.

Group AMPs, SORT, Eliminating Duplicate Rows, and No Residual Conditions (group_amps)
- The operation is a group AMP operation, meaning that it occurs on more than 1, but fewer than all, AMPs in the system.

sort
- A sort operation occurs.

eliminating duplicate rows
- Duplicate rows can exist in spool files, either as a result of selecting non-unique columns from any table or of selecting from a MULTISET table. This process signifies "distinct" processing where sets are redistributed and sorted by value (by "sort key" or by "row hash and sort key" together) to

eliminate duplicate rows as opposed to aggregate processing (via a "SUM Step") which may also be used to retrieve a "distinct" list of values..

no residual conditions
- Rows are selected in their entirety; there are no specific search conditions.
- All applicable conditions have been applied to the rows.

Last Use, End Transaction, and Computed Globally

Here are some common Explain phrases.

(Last Use)
- This term identifies the last reference to a spool file that contains intermediate data that produces a statement's final result.
- The spool file is released following this step.

END TRANSACTION step
- This indicates that processing is complete and that any locks on the data may be released, and the Transient Journal images are released.

computed globally
- The computation involves all the intermediate spool file data.

By skipping global aggregation
- When a unique column is included in a multicolumn collect statistics command, the database can avoid the cost of redistributing rows and aggregating them globally.

(no lock required)
- The lock that is required for the step was acquired earlier in the process.

Teradata 14 Solutions Development

Chapter 6: Practice Questions

1. Where should outer join condition or filter condition be specified?
    a. The FROM clause.
    b. The ON clause.
    c. The WHERE clause.

2. Which statement best describes an outer join?
    a. Only matching rows are returned.
    b. Only non-matching rows are returned.
    c. Matching rows and non-matching rows are returned.

3. Which is the join that doesn't always use all of the AMPs?
    a. Merge join
    b. Product join
    c. Hash join
    d. Nested join
    e. Exclusion join

4. Before two rows can be joined, _____.
    a. they must be on the same AMP
    b. they must be from the same table
    c. they must be copied to spool first.

5. Any join can be accomplished as a _____ join.
    a. Merge
    b. Product
    c. Nested
    d. ROWID

6. Which of the following can be EXPLAINed?
    a. EXPLAIN
    b. Macros
    c. Stored Procedures

Chapter Notes

Utilize this space for notes, key points to remember, diagrams, areas of further study, etc.

Chapter 7 - Utilities

Certification Objectives

- ✓ Given a scenario, identify which load utility should be used.
- ✓ Given a scenario, identify the appropriate export option.
- ✓ Given a scenario, identify the locking impact caused by the different load utilities.
- ✓ Given a scenario, identify load strategies for availability and data integrity.
- ✓ Identify considerations when loading BLOBs and CLOBs.
- ✓ Describe the effect of various FastLoad/MultiLoad parameters.
- ✓ Describe the effect of various BTEQ parameters.
- ✓ Describe the effect of various Teradata Parallel Transporter parameters.
- ✓ Identify the different methods utilities use to handle duplicate rows.
- ✓ Identify how to eliminate unwanted duplicate rows from a multi-set table.
- ✓ Identify how to load set and multi-set tables.
- ✓ Identify possible client performance considerations of MultiLoad and TPump.
- ✓ Describe the effect of various TPump performance parameters.

Before You Begin

You should be familiar with the following terms and concepts.

Terms	Key Concepts
FastLoad/TPT Load Operator	Similarities and differences
MultiLoad/TPT Update Operator	Similarities and differences
BTEQ/TPT SQL	Similarities and differences

Teradata 14 Solutions Development

Terms	Key Concepts
Operator	
TPump/TPT Stream Operator	Similarities and differences
FastExport/TPT Export Operator	Similarities and differences

There are various strategies and reasons (for and against) regarding the best approaches for loading data. Therefore, it is extremely important that the development teams are on the same page in regards to these strategies.

Once confirmed, these strategies should become part of a check list that the DBAs, Developers and Operations personnel adhere to every time they develop a load process. It is of the utmost importance that these conventions are adopted when loading tables in Teradata. This chapter discusses the different tools and options that can be utilized for loading data into Teradata.

BTEQ

BTEQ is an abbreviation of Basic Teradata Query. It is a command-based program that enables users to connect to and submit SQL queries to the Teradata Database. BTEQ also provides several format options to return data (i.e. screen, flat file, or printer). Lastly, when used, it is intended for "row-hash" update access (i.e. hash level inserts, updates, and deletes) to tables of relatively low access having little or no request failures.

A BTEQ session provides a quick and easy way to access a Teradata Database. In a BTEQ session, you can do the following:

- Establish one or more sessions on the database to submit SQL requests.
- Enter Teradata SQL statements to view, add, modify, and delete data.
- Create columnar reports that are formatted via various commands.
- Enter operating system commands.
- Create and use database objects like Teradata stored procedures, macros, and UDFs.
- Load "clean" data from files very quickly (using ARRAY processing via PACK)

BTEQ operates in both batch and interactive modes:

- In interactive mode, you start a BTEQ session, and then interactively submit commands to the database.
- In batch mode, you prepare BTEQ and submit scripts to BTEQ for processing.

When you logon to BTEQ, the default is to send your SQL through a single session. However, BTEQ can log on to Teradata sessions in sets so that a number of sessions can run in parallel within a given set. This is especially helpful when you need to process a high volume of repetitive tasks whose order does not matter, such as loading a large number of rows onto a database. In this case, having a number of parallel sessions with each handling some of the requests can substantially speed up operations.

Though BTEQ can support a maximum of 200 sessions, the actual maximum depends on the configuration of your system and your terminal or workstation. The maximum for your system could be less than 200, and as few as 16 for PC workstations.

You can substantially speed up certain kinds of load operations when logging multiple SESSIONS prior to the LOGON command. The default number of sessions is 1, as stated above.

Through the use of the .IMPORT command, you can specify a data file to be used as input.

Transactions and BTEQ

BTEQ (client) has one purpose: to identify a request and send it to the server. As a line-by-line interpreter, BTEQ parses each coded line looking for a semicolon as the last character. If it finds a semicolon as the last, non-space, character (comment is considered character text), it sends each and every previous line not ending with a semicolon as the request. It sends the request to Teradata and awaits a response before sending the next request. Any semicolons appearing elsewhere in the request (that are not at the end of a line) are ignored.

BTEQ handles Request Parcels, which may contain 1 or more SQL statements. If certain errors occur, and RETRY is ON (the default), BTEQ will resend the failing request parcel. BTEQ only has RETRY logic, not RESTART logic.

You can create multi-statement requests by proper semicolon placement in your BTEQ script, or you can put the SQL statements in a macro and have BTEQ execute the macro.

You can speed up BTEQ by specifying QUIET ON. If you use the QUIET command with the REPEAT or = command, BTEQ determines the reporting of time statistics by the number of sessions being run. With multiple sessions, BTEQ only reports the summary times for each cycle (start time, finish time, and total time). During a single session, BTEQ reports summary and processing times of queries executed in each cycle.

Typically, the QUIET and REPEAT commands are used together in multi-session data-load operations.

FastLoad

Fastload is a "checkpoint-restart" (batch) utility that does not use the Transient Journal. It uses its own scripting language, has its own protocol, and is used to load (insert only) empty tables. It performs duplicate row elimination on both SET and MULTISET tables.

You can load data from:

- Channel-attached disk or files from tape on a client system
- Network-attached PC workstation files
- INMOD routines to preprocess input data
- External devices with source data properly setup for loading

By utilizing multiple sessions to load data, Fastload can increase the throughput for loading operations. However, Fastload can only load data to one table per job. If you want to load data into more than one table in the Teradata Database, you must submit multiple Teradata FastLoad jobs - one for each table.

Full tape support is not available for any function in Teradata FastLoad for network attached client systems. If you want to load data from a tape device, you will need to build a custom access module that communicates with the device.

When you invoke Teradata FastLoad, the utility executes the control commands and along with the SQL statements in your Teradata FastLoad job script. During this operation, the following is done:

1. Logs you on to the Teradata Database with the defined specified number of sessions with your username, password, and tdpid/acctid information.
2. Loads the data into the table on the Teradata Database.
3. Logs you off from the Teradata Database.
4. If successful, the FastLoad utility will return the following information:

   - Total records read, skipped, and delivered to the database
   - Number of errors inserted FastLoad error tables
   - Number of rows inserted and applied
   - Count of duplicate rows

As noted above, the table getting loaded with data must be empty and cannot have any secondary indexes defined. In addition, FastLoad does not load duplicate rows (i.e. where every value has the exact same data across all columns of an existing row.) This rule also applies to MULTISET tables. If you want to load duplicate rows, you will have MultiLoad with a MULTISET table.

On network-attached workstations, Teradata FastLoad uses the TCP/IP network protocol for all data transfer operations.

On channel-attached systems, Teradata FastLoad transfers data as either:

- A multi-volume data set or file
- A number of single-volume data sets or files in separate Teradata FastLoad jobs

You can restart serial Teradata FastLoad operations by loading the next tape in a series instead of beginning with the first tape in a set.

In either case, Teradata FastLoad:

UTILITIES

- Uses multiple Teradata sessions, at one session per AMP, to transfer data
- Transfers multiple rows of data within a single message

Until you complete the Teradata FastLoad job and have loaded the data into the Teradata FastLoad table:

- There is no journaling or fallback data
- You cannot define the secondary indexes
- Join indexes, hash indexes, or foreign key references are not allowed until the load is completed

Restarting FastLoad

A FastLoad job that has been stopped before completing during a load or end-load phase of the operation is considered to be in a paused state. This condition can be unintentional, intentional, or can be a system failure or error condition.

To pause a job intentionally, use the LOGOFF or QUIT command before the END LOADING command in your script. Unintentional conditions to pause a job are as follows:

- Client workstation or FastLoad failures
- Conditions that cause unrecoverable errors
- Database or table errors
- Database failures

Note: While in a paused state, the target table and the error tables are locked on the database. You cannot access the table until the Fastload job completes; that is, the data is not available until the job is finished.

Restart Procedures

The procedure that you use to restart a paused FastLoad job is dependent on the phase of the job when it was paused.

- You can restart a job that was paused during loading, either from the beginning, or from the most recent checkpoint if the checkpoint option was specified in the BEGIN LOADING command.

- You can also restart a job that was paused during the end-loading phase. This is because checkpointing is done internally by the database in this phase. You generally do not need to do anything in this case because processing after the END LOADING command is executed on the database and does not depend on the FastLoad utility.

To restart the job if paused during the loading phase

1. Remove the CREATE TABLE, DROP TABLE and DELETE statements from the FastLoad job script. You do not want your restarted job to drop the partially loaded FastLoad table or delete the entries in the two error tables.

2. Restart the Teradata FastLoad to start the job. The Teradata FastLoad utility:

   - New sessions are created with the LOGON command.
   - Establishes the restart point by reading the restart.
   - The BEGIN LOADING command will notate that the job will be restarted.

Note: If a load is using an INMOD routine, the INMOD routine (when restarted) needs to be able to handle restarts and checkpoints. During this restart, the FastLoad job will display a status code of 2 or 4 in a load operation. The INMOD routine will modify the record to read the position of the last checkpoint and then send these data records to be loaded.

To restart the job if paused during the end loading phase

1. The same LOGON command must be used as in the previous job.

2. Use BEGIN LOADING and END LOADING commands, as outlined in the following example:

```
LOGON dbc/sjn,music ;
BEGIN LOADING Fast_Table
ERRORFILES Error_1, Error_2 ;
END LOADING ;
```

Figure 7.1

Note: If you use your FastLoad job script to CREATE, DROP, or DELETE, these commands need to be before restarting the job.

FastExport

Teradata FastExport is a command-driven utility that enables you to unload large quantities of data from tables or views on a Teradata Database. You can export data from any object (i.e. tables, views) as long as you have the SELECT privilege.

The exported data can be offloaded via the following methods:

- To a flat file located on a network-attached PC workstation or channel-attached system.

- The Output Modification (OUTMOD) routine is an optional command that enables you to preprocess and verify the exported data before it is stored.

When you invoke FastExport, the utility executes the control commands and SQL statements in the job script. These instruct FastExport to do the following:

1. Logs you on to the database with your defined number of sessions, tdpid/acctid, username, and password for the script.
2. Access the data from the Teradata Database with your defined SQL Statement based on your format requirements.
3. Execute any OUTMOD routine defined to preprocess the data and export the data to the destination file.
4. Log you off the database

Note: FastExport now has a NOSPOOL option.

Restarting FastExport

A FastExport job that has been stopped before completing during an offload operation, where the restart log table has not been dropped, can be restarted. This condition can be unintentional, intentional, or can be a system failure or error condition.

Unintentional conditions to pause a job are as follows:

- Job script error
- Hardware failures
- Software errors

FastExport can restart some jobs that are stopped automatically. However, and in most cases, jobs will have to be manually restarted.

UTILITIES

To manually restart the job, resubmit the entire job making sure that the same restart log table is used.

Once restarted, the FastExport utility will do the following:

1. Reestablish sessions specified in job
2. Access and reads the restart log table to establish the restart point
3. Resumes processing the job script

After a Job Script Error

When an error occurs in a job script, it creates an error message and returns an error code. From there, you can access the job script and make modifications to resolve the problem. Once completed, you can resubmit the job. FastExport will restart based on the last completed statement that was recorded in the restart log.

After Hardware Failures or Software Error Conditions

Automatic restarts of jobs will occur after some hardware failures, software errors, and after system recovery. These include:

- Down AMP
- CLIv2 errors on your PC workstation
- Network failures
- Nonrecoverable I/O error
- Database restarts

If the failure occurred with a *single* select request, then FastExport will resume processing when the system recovery is completed and by resubmitting a single select request.

If the failure occurred with *multiple* select requests, then FastExport will resume processing after system recovery is completed and by resubmitting the last select statement before the failure occurred based on the restart log.

MultiLoad

MultiLoad is a "checkpoint-restart" (batch) utility that does not use the Transient Journal. It uses its own scripting language, has its own protocol (not TJ based), and is used to update (insert, update, delete, upsert) empty or populated tables. It allows duplicate rows for MULTISET tables. A single MultiLoad job can perform several different import and delete tasks on database tables and views:

- Import tasks can do INSERTs, and UPDATEs functions on up to five different tables or views.
- A Delete task can remove large numbers of rows from a single table.

You can import data from the following:

- Disk or tape files from a channel-attached client system, which requires a customer access module.
- Files from a network-attached PC workstation.
- Input modules (INMOD) can be utilized to preprocess and validate data before loaded.
- Utilize access modules to connect to other database for loading
- Other device providing source data

Note: In order to load and perform maintenance tasks with MultiLoad, you must have the appropriate access rights.

Multiload does have some restrictions and limitations. For example, the table(s) you are going to load with Multiload cannot have any USI's, referential integrity, or defined triggers. In addition, Multiload

UTILITIES

does not support loading into a NOPI table. However, NUSi's are allowed.

Just like the Fastlaod, Multiload has two primary loading phases which are as follows:

- **Acquisition Phase** – Data from the input stream is hash-distributed to the appropriate AMPs. When all of the input records have been read and sent to the AMPs, they are then sorted into row hash sequence and written to a work table. The target table is still available to the users during this phase.

- **Application Phase** – The system upgrades the lock to a Write lock. The sorted input records are applied to the table using the appropriate DML command(s). Each target data block is read into memory just once and all changes are applied to it at that time. When the phase successfully ends, the work tables are dropped during a subsequent cleanup phase. During the APPLY phase, each updated block becomes a checkpoint for restartability.

- Any NUSI row changes for each are written to a separate subtable during primary data row changes. After the primary table data changes are finished, each subtable of NUSI changes are sorted and applied in turn.

Restarting a Paused MultiLoad Job

A MultiLoad job that has been stopped before completing a load operation, and is still in the acquisition phase of the MultiLoad operation, can be restarted. This condition can be unintentional, intentional, or can be a system failure or error condition.

Teradata 14 Solutions Development

You can pause a MultiLoad job intentionally by using a PAUSE ACQUISITION command between the BEGIN MLOAD and END MLOAD commands in the MultiLoad job script.

Unintentional conditions to pause a job are as follows:

- A MultiLoad job script error
- An unrecoverable I/O error
- A system that is in down AMP recovery status
- Database restarts
- Job aborts
- Client system failures

Note: MultiLoad permits non-exclusive access to target tables from other users except during the Application Phase. However, once in the acquisition phase, you must have an ACCESS lock to read the table.

After Using the PAUSE ACQUISITION Command

To restart a job that is in a paused state caused by a PAUSE ACQUISITION command, do the following:

1. Remove the PAUSE ACQUISITION command from the job script.
2. Restart the MultiLoad job.

Once done, MultiLoad will do the following:

1. Reestablishes sessions specified in the job
2. Access and reads the restart log table to establish the restart point
3. Resumes processing the job script

After a MultiLoad Job Script Error

When an error occurs in a job script, it creates an error message and returns an error code. From there, you can access the job script and

UTILITIES

make modifications to resolve the problem. Once completed, you can resubmit the job. MultiLoad will restart based on the last completed statement that was recorded in the restart log.

After an Unrecoverable I/O Error

When experiencing an unrecoverable I/O error while accessing a fallback type table, MultiLoad will automatically attempt to restart the job script.

Note: Some I/O errors can cause an AMP to stop participating in a job. In this case, the job will stop with error messages. In addition, if you are conducting a restart operation, error messages may occur as well.

After a Down AMP is Recovered

When MultiLoad is recovered from a down AMP situation and an error occurs on a worktable with fallback on the restart, this could indicate that additional procedures will be required to recover the table.

After a Teradata Database Restart

MultiLoad will automatically restart after the normal recovery operation such database restart. In this case, no intervention is required for this job. However, if the work tables or error tables are mistakenly dropped or missing, the job will abort with an error message.

After a Teradata Database System Reconfiguration

If a MultiLoad job is active and the Reconfiguration program is invoked, you could encounter problems where the error tables are not redistributed. When MultiLoad restarts after the reconfiguration is completed, the MultiLoad script will fail with errors.

In this scenario, when MultiLoad attempts to restart, the following error message will occur:

```
UTY0805 DBC failure, 2563: MLOAD not allowed: DBC had been reconfigured.
```

When this occurs, the tables being loaded cannot be recovered and the target tables must be reloaded.

Note: Do not reconfigure the Teradata Database during an active MultiLoad job.

After a Job Abort or Client System Failure

If the job was halted before or after the application phase due to client failure or an abort command, then you can restart the job as long as no changes were made to the job script. MultiLoad will utilize the restart log table to determine where to resume the job.

Note: If you modify tables or databases that are involved in a multi-step job, you may corrupt them.

TPump

TPump is meant to be used as a streaming, transaction based, (uses the Transient Journal) utility. It uses its own scripting language, but does adhere to transaction protocol on the server side, and checkpoint-restart on the client side. As with transaction processing, the locking levels are determined at the request-level.

TPump, unlike MultiLoad, is a low-volume batch utility tool that can load and perform maintenance on several tables simultaneously. To achieve this, TPump uses native SQL commands to load or maintain data at low, medium, and high rates into the Teradata Database.

Throttles such as using multiple sessions and multi-statement requests are utilized to handle the throughput.

TPump achieves this near real-time processing by continuously streaming data into the data warehouse, rather than through traditional batch updates. Continuous loads are achieved by accessing data from the client system in low volumes. The result is more accurate and timely data.

The key difference from FastLoad, and MultiLoad is that TPump uses row hash locks where the other utilities use table level locks. This enables TPump to simultaneously load data while users are running queries. This feature also enables TPump to be stopped at any time with no failures.

As indicated, the throttling feature which enables TPump to stream when the business is utilizing the system, or load like MultiLoad during batch windows, is a dynamic and key benefit of this utility.

TPump can not only throttle the number of statements to run per minute, you can also determine the amount of data that will be processed per minute. TPump's main benefits include:

- TPump does not require data staging, files, or custom hardware.
- Jobs restart with no interaction. They can run during database restarts, and network slowdowns.
- TPump can transform data in-flight before loading it to Teradata.
- TPump supports native SQL and conditional logic statements, making it unnecessary to customize the utility.
- TPump also has several performance parameters available with such as robust on, serialize on, and defining the KEY for loading.

Recovering an Aborted TPump Job

A TPump job that has been stopped before completing a load operation (i.e. database space, abort commands, UNIX kernel panic, error limits exceeded), can be restarted providing the database objects, the restart log table, the error table, and DML macros have not been changed.

Note: An aborted TPump job can be restarted if the same job script is utilized in which case, TPump will perform the recovery.

Recovering from Script Errors

When an error occurs in a job script, it creates an error message and returns an error code. From there, you can access the job script and make modifications to resolve the problem. Once completed, you can resubmit the job. Tpump will restart based on the last completed statement that was recorded in the restart log.

Teradata Parallel Transporter

Teradata Parallel Transporter is a client software product that is of an object oriented nature and uses a single SQL-like script language to accomplish tasks that were done using the traditional ('standalone') utilities of FastLoad, MultiLoad, FastExport, and TPump. Jobs are run using 'producer' operators and 'consumer' operators which define the type of task (load or unload) to be performed. Additionally, TPT functionality can be extended via 3rd party products and/or customizations. Teradata Parallel Transporter can be used to load data from a variety of inputs or sources as well as for exporting data to external targets.

UTILITIES

TPT can be invoked via a script, or it can be activated by an API (Application Program Interface). There is also a GUI-based **TPT Wizard** which can be used for script generation.

Major Features of TPT

The following are principal features of TPT:

- **Single Script Language**
  This simplifies the creation of load/unload operations.
- **Complex 'Multi-Step' Load Scenarios**
  A TPT script can contain multiple job steps, each of which may be performing a load or unload function.
- **Increased Throughput**
  TPT permits multiple instances of each operator in a script, thereby eliminating the single input stream of the traditional utilities.
- **Direct API**
  The Application Program Interface (API) allows customers and vendors to write programs to directly load or unload Teradata tables using C or C++.
- **Reduced File Storage**
  TPT eliminates the need for intermediate file storage by holding data in data buffers (called 'streams').

TPT integrates the traditional utilities (FastLoad, MultiLoad, TPump, and FastExport) into one platform using a single scripting language that uses 'operators'. To load a table, you now invoke a 'load' operator instead of running FastLoad. To update a table, you invoke an 'update' operator instead of running MultiLoad, and so on. Each operator can, of course, use multiple user sessions for additional parallelism.

Additional TPT Features

Teradata Parallel Transporter replaces the former Teradata Warehouse Builder. It uses the same script language so migration from TWB to TPT is seamless.

Here are some of the features of TPT:

- Concurrent Load from Multiple Sources
    - TPT can simultaneously load data from multiple and dissimilar sources in a single job.
    - It can execute multiple instances of an operator.
    - It can export, transform, and load one or more tables in a single job.
    - It can perform in-line filtering and transformation of data.
- Improved Performance through Parallelism and Scalability
    - TPT automatically distributes input and output data into data streams.
    - Data is streamed between operators without being written to disk.
    - Each data stream can be shared with multiple instances of the operators.
- Checkpoint Restart
    - TPT can automatically resume load jobs from the last checkpoint if the job aborts.
- Directory Scan
    - Permits multiple files in a client directory to be simultaneously processed as source data.
- Improved Throughput
    - Overcome input file I/O and CPU bottlenecks with multiple operator instances, as opposed to single-threaded applications such as MultiLoad or FastLoad.

UTILITIES

The following diagram illustrates the Teradata PT architecture. The three tiers represent source, load, and target environments, which can either reside on different servers or on the same server.

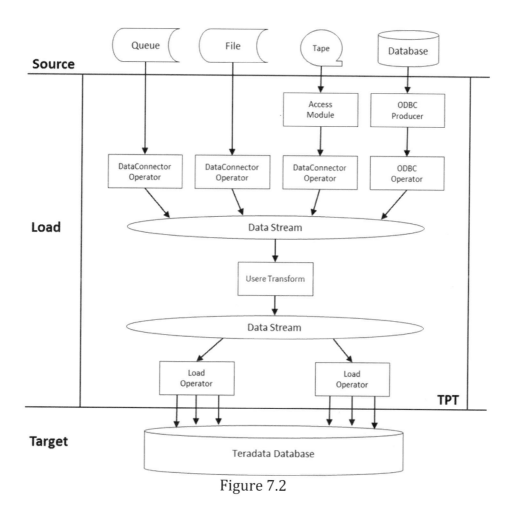

Figure 7.2

TPT achieves pipeline parallelism by connecting operator instances through data streams.

Teradata 14 Solutions Development

The following chart shows the major components of a TPT job.

COMPONENT	FUNCTION
Input Sources	These can be databases (both relational and non-relational) or database servers, data storage devices (i.e. tape or DVD readers), file objects, such as images, pictures, voice, text, etc.
Producer Operators	These extract data from a source and write it to a data stream. They 'produce' a data stream.
Data Stream	A data buffer in memory used to temporarily hold data. A data stream can accept data from multiple producer instances, and can distribute the data to multiple consumer operator instances.
Consumer Operators	These accept data from a data stream. They 'consume' the data and write it to the output target.
Output Target	These can be databases (both relational and non-relational) or database servers, data storage devices. For a load operator, the target must be a Teradata database.

Figure 7.3

UTILITIES

The following chart shows the differences between TPT and the stand-alone utilities.

Operator	Standalone Equivalent	Purpose
DataConnector operator	Data Connector (PIOM)	Read data from and write data to flat files
DataConnector operator with WebSphere MQ Access Module	Data Connector (PIOM)	Read data from IBM WebSphere MQ
DataConnector operator with Named Pipes Access Module	Data Connector (PIOM)	Read data from a named pipe
DDL operator	BTEQ	Execute DDL, DCL, and self-contained DML SQL statements
Export operator	FastExport	High-volume export of data from Teradata Database
FastExport OUTMOD Adapter operator	FastExport OUTMOD Routine	Preprocess exported data with a FastExport OUTMOD routine before writing the data to a file
FastLoad INMOD Adapter Operator	FastLoad INMOD Routine	Read and preprocess data from a FastLoad INMOD data source
Load Operator	FastLoad	High-volume load of an empty table
MultiLoad INMOD Adapter Operator	MultiLoad INMOD Routine	Read and preprocess data from a MultiLoad INMOD data source
ODBC operator	OLE DB Access Module	Export data from any non-Teradata database that has an

Operator	Standalone Equivalent	Purpose
		ODBC driver
OS Command operator	Client host operating system	Execute host operating system commands
SQL Inserter operator	BTEQ	Insert data into a Teradata table using SQL protocol
SQL Selector operator	BTEQ	Select data from a Teradata table using SQL protocol
Stream operator	TPump	Continuous loading of Teradata tables using SQL protocol
Update operator	MultiLoad	Update, insert, and delete rows

Figure 7.4

In addition to producer and consumer operators, TPT also has filter operators and standalone operators.

The follow chart summarizes the operators and their characteristics.

OPERATOR TYPE	FUNCTION
Producer Operators They *Produce* a Data Stream	1. Get data from the Teradata database or an external data source. 2. Write the data to a data stream. 3. Typically make the data available to other operators.
Consumer Operators They *Consume* a Data Stream	1. Typically receive data from other operators. 2. Read data from a data stream. 3. Load data into a Teradata database or external data store.
Filter Operators	Perform data selection, data validation, data cleansing, and data condensing.

UTILITIES

OPERATOR TYPE	FUNCTION
They *Consume* and *Produce* Data Streams	Filter operators function as both consumers and producers since they consume an input stream, handle the data, and then produce an output data stream.
Standalone Operators No Data Stream action	1. Used for submitting DDL commands. 2. Also used for doing Delete Tasks (functioning as an update operator). 3. Do not depend on input data from any sources other than the job script. 4. Do not send or receive data from other operators – no data streams.

Figure 7.5

CHECKPOINT AND RESTART

Export operator

The Export operator behaves differently from other Teradata PT operators in that it does not support a user-defined restart log table. Instead, it takes a checkpoint only when all data is sent to the data stream. If a restart occurs, the Export operator with either send all or none of the data based on whether a checkpoint has taken place.

DDL operator

If a restart occurs due to an abnormal termination, the DDL operator will go to the beginning SQL statement for that group. However, if the group has only one SQL statement, the DDL operator will start at that statement.

Because SQL statements are sent in the order in which they are specified in the APPLY statement for that group. The DDL operator can take a checkpoint after each group is executed. As noted, a group can contain one or more SQL statements. If a checkpoint is used for a

DDL operator, it will mark the last group of DDL/DML SQL statements it executed successfully.

If a restart and the last request was successful, the DDL operator can resume to the next step. However, if the last request fails before the restart, then the DDL operator will start at the last failed request.

Load operator

Teradata PT can automatically resume load jobs from the last checkpoint if the job aborts.

Update operator

When changes are applied to target table(s) in the application phase with an UPDATE operator, it cannot be rolled back. Therefore, it can only move forward and cannot be returned to its original state. It is recommended that you archive these tables before running an UPDATE operation.

Stream operator

Checkpoints are taken by default at the start of and at the end of STREAM operations, unless a checkpoint is specified. Checkpoints can be user-defined to provide granular restartability for longer running jobs (i.e. minutes or seconds.)

Utility Limits

The setting of two control fields, *MaxLoadTasks* and *MaxLoadAWT*, affects how many utilities can run concurrently.

UTILITIES

The MaxLoadTasks field specifies the combined number of FastLoad, MultiLoad, and FastExport tasks (jobs), and their TPT counterparts, that are allowed to run concurrently on Teradata Database.

Throttle rules for load utility concurrency are done via TASM or TIWM along with determining if we are working with either SLES10 vs SLES11. For SLES10, there are options for Workload Management to deploy this. For example, if TASM is enabled, you are subject to the utility limits in the rule-set unless the DBSControl field is set to ignore the TASM session/job limits.

AMP Worker Tasks (AWTs) are processes (threads on some platforms) dedicated to servicing the database work requests. A Teradata Database has a fixed number of AWTs that were defined during system initialization. Each AWT looks for a work request to arrive in the Teradata Database system, services the request, and then looks for another. An AWT can process requests of any work type.

The number of AWTs required by FastLoad and MultiLoad changes as their jobs run. More AWTs are required in the early phases of the jobs than in the later phases. Teradata Database dynamically calculates the total AWTs required by active jobs, and allows more jobs to start as AWTs become available.

The following chart shows the different number of required AWTs at different phases of execution for FastLoad and MultiLoad.

Load Utility Phase	Number of AWTs Required
FastLoad: Loading	3
FastLoad: End Loading	1
MultiLoad: Acquisition	2
MultiLoad: Application	1 per target table

Figure 7.6

If MaxLoadAWT is greater than zero, new FastLoad and MultiLoad jobs are rejected when the MaxLoadAWT limit is reached, regardless of the MaxLoadTasks setting. Therefore, FastLoad and MultiLoad jobs may be rejected before the MaxLoadTasks limit is reached.

Here is how the MaxLoadTasks field works together with the MaxLoadAWT field.

If MaxLoadAWT is zero (the default):

- MaxLoadTasks can be an integer from zero through 15.
- The MaxLoadTasks field specifies the maximum number of combined FastLoad, MultiLoad, and FastExport jobs that can run concurrently.
- The system does not consider the number of available AWTs when limiting the number of load utilities that can run concurrently.

If MaxLoadAWT is greater than zero:

- MaxLoadTasks is an integer from zero through 30.
- The MaxLoadTasks field sets the maximum number of combined FastLoad and MultiLoad jobs that can run concurrently. MaxLoadTasks does not directly limit the number of FastExport jobs that can run.
- The number of combined FastLoad and MultiLoad jobs that can run concurrently is limited by the values of both the MaxLoadTasks field and the MaxLoadAWT field. When either limit is met, no further FastLoad or MultiLoad jobs are allowed to start until the limiting factor is reduced.
- The maximum number of load utility jobs of any type— FastLoad, MultiLoad, or FastExport—that can run concurrently is 60. Consequently, the number of FastExport jobs allowed to run at any time is 60 minus the number of combined FastLoad and MultiLoad jobs that are running.

UTILITIES

- If MaxLoadAWT is set to anything greater than zero, it can only be reset to zero if MaxLoadTasks is 15 or less.

Parameters

BTEQ

The following is a list of the BTEQ commands:

=	NULL
ABORT	OMIT
AUTOKEYRETRIEVE	OS
CMS	PACK
COMPILE	PAGEBREAK
DECIMALDIGITS	PAGELENGTH
DEFAULTS	QUIET
ECHOREQ	QUIT
ENCRYPTION	RECORDMODE
ERRORLEVEL	REMARK
ERROROUT	REPEAT
EXIT	REPEATSTOP
EXPORT	RETCANCEL
EXPORTEJECT	RETLIMIT
FOLDLINE	RETRY
FOOTING	RTITLE
FORMAT	RUN
FORMCHAR	SEPARATOR
FULLYEAR	SESSION CHARSET
GOTO	SESSION RESPBUFLEN
HANG	SESSION SQLFLAG
HEADING	SESSION TRANSACTION
HELP BTEQ	SESSION TWORESPBUFS
HX	SESSIONS
IF...THEN ...	SHOW CONTROLS
IMPORT	SHOW ERRORMAP

INDICDATA	SHOW VERSIONS
LABEL	SIDETITLES
LARGEDATAMODE	SKIPDOUBLE
LOGDATA	SKIPLINE
LOGMECH	SUPPRESS
LOGOFF	TDP
LOGON	TIMEMSG
LOGONPROMPT	TITLEDASHES
MAXERROR	TSO
MESSAGEOUT	UNDERLINE
NOTIFY	WIDTH

Figure 7.7

FASTLOAD

The following is a list of the FastLoad commands:

AXSMOD	LOGON
BEGIN LOADING	NOTIFY
CLEAR	OS
DATEFORM	QUIT
DEFINE	RECORD
END LOADING	RUN
ERRLIMIT	SESSIONS
HELP	SET RECORD
HELP TABLE	SET SESSION CHARSET
INSERT	SHOW
LOGDATA	SHOW VERSIONS
LOGMECH	SLEEP
LOGOFF	TENACITY

Figure 7.8

UTILITIES

FASTEXPORT

The following is a list of the FastExport commands:

ACCEPT	LAYOUT
BEGIN EXPORT	LOGDATA
DATEFORM	LOGMECH
DISPLAY	LOGOFF
END EXPORT	LOGON
EXPORT	LOGTABLE.
FIELD	ROUTE MESSAGES
FILLER	RUN FILE
IF, ELSE, and ENDIF	SET
IMPORT	SYSTEM

Figure 7.9

MULTILOAD

The following is a list of the MultiLoad commands:

ACCEPT	LOGDATA
BEGIN MLOAD—Import Task	LOGMECH
BEGIN DELETE MLOAD—Delete Task	LOGOFF
DATEFORM	LOGON
DELETE	LOGTABLE
DISPLAY	PAUSE ACQUISITION
DML LABEL	RELEASE MLOAD
END MLOAD	ROUTE MESSAGES
FIELD	RUN FILE
FILLER	SET
IF, ELSE, and ENDIF	SYSTEM
IMPORT	TABLE
INSERT	UPDATE
LAYOUT	

Figure 7.10

TPUMP

The following is a list of the TPump command:

ACCEPT	LAYOUT
BEGIN LOAD	LOGDATA
DATABASE	LOGMECH
DATEFORM	LOGOFF
DELETE	LOGON
DISPLAY	LOGTABLE
DML	NAME
END LOAD	PARTITION
EXECUTE	ROUTE
FIELD	RUN FILE
FILLER	SET
IF, ELSE, and ENDIF	SYSTEM
IMPORT	TABLE
INSERT	UPDATE

Figure 7.11

TPT

The following is a list of the TPT commands and their parameters:

COMMAND	PARAMETERS
tbuild	-f *filename* *jobname* -d -D -e *characterset* -l *latencyInterval* -m *statisticsInterval* -n -r *checkpointDirectory* -R *restartLimit*

UTILITIES

COMMAND	PARAMETERS

	-s *jobstepIdentifier*
	 -S -------
	   DD:ddname
	   dsname
	   sysoutClass
	 -t
	 -u *jobAttributes*
	 -v *filename*
	 -V *versionnumber*
	 -z *checkpointInterval*

Tlogview	-j *jobid*
	 -l *logFilename*
	
	 -e *characterset*
	 -f --------
	   fromList
	   "*" -g
	   TWB_STATUS
	   TWB_SRCTGT
	 -h
	 -o *outputFilename*
	 -p
	 -v *logviewFormat*
	 -w *whereClause*

Job-Level Commands twbcmd *jobname*	------------ JOB CHECKPOINT JOB PAUSE JOB RESTART JOB RESUME JOB STATUS JOB TERMINATE

COMMAND	PARAMETERS
Operator-Level Commands twbcmd *jobName operatorCommandId*	rate= *statementRate* rate= unlimited periodicity= *periodicity*
twbkill	*jobname*
Twbrmcp	*userid jobname*
Twbstat	

Figure 7.12

The following is a list of the Teradata PT Statements:

APPLY DEFINE DBMS DEFINE JOB DEFINE OPERATOR	DEFINE SCHEMA DEFINE TABLE DEFINE TABLE SET

Figure 7.13

The following is a list of the Teradata PT Operators:

DATACONNECTOR Operator DDL Operator EXPORT Operator FastExport OUTMOD Adapter Operator FastLoad INMOD Adapter Operator LOAD Operator MultiLoad INMOD Adapter Operator	ODBC Operator OS Command Operator SQL Inserter Operator SQL Selector Operator STREAM Operator UPDATE Operator

Figure 7.14

CLOBs and BLOBs

BTEQ
If an attempt is made to retrieve a row of data that exceeds 65,473 bytes for workstation builds or 64,260 bytes for mainframe builds and exported to a file, the request is aborted with an error. However, if you use the command *.SET LARGEDATAMODE ON* and send the data to standard out, BTEQ does not impose any size limits.

FASTLOAD
BLOB and CLOB are not supported by FASTLOAD

FASTEXPORT
BLOB and CLOB are not supported by FASTEXPORT

MULTILOAD
BLOB and CLOB are not supported by MULTILOAD

TPUMP
BLOB and CLOB are not supported by TPUMP

TPT
The Export Operator cannot handle Character Large Object (CLOB) or Binary Large Object (BLOB) data type. However, the SQL Selector Operator can handle CLOB/BLOB data. The TPT Wizard cannot handle CLOBs or BLOBs. Do not select any tables containing them.

PRIMARY INDEXES
Primary index columns cannot have data types of BLOB or CLOB.

SECONDARY INDEXES
You cannot include columns having BLOB or CLOB data types in any secondary index definition.

Client performance considerations

GENERAL

Notify exit routine

A notify exit routine specifies a predefined action to be performed whenever certain significant events occur during a Teradata FastLoad job. Notify exit routines are especially useful in operator-free environments where job scheduling relies heavily on automation to optimize system performance.

INMOD & OUTMOD Addressing Mode on VM and MVS Systems

Use either 31-bit or 24-bit addressing for INMOD routines on channel-attached systems.

The 31-bit mode provides access to more memory, which enhances performance for Teradata FastLoad jobs with a large number of sessions.

Use the following linkage parameters to specify the addressing mode when building INMOD routines for VM and MVS systems:

- AMODE(31) for 31-bit addressing
- AMODE(24) for 24-bit addressing

Sessions

There is no general method to determine the optimal number of sessions, because it is dependent on several factors, including, but not limited to:

- Teradata Database performance and workload
- Client platform type, performance, and workload

- Channel performance, for channel-attached systems
- Network topology and performance, for network-attached systems
- Volume of data to be processed by the application

Using too few sessions is likely to unnecessarily limit throughput. On the other hand, using too many sessions can increase session management overhead (and also reduce the number of sessions available to other applications) and may, in some circumstances, degrade throughput.

Regardless of the size of the Teradata Database configuration, for large repetitive production applications, it will usually be appropriate to experiment with several different session configurations to determine the best trade-off between resource utilization and throughput performance.

For larger Teradata Database configurations, it is appropriate to establish an installation default for the maximum number of sessions that is less than one session per AMP. This can be done either via the installation configuration file or via a standard runtime parameter. An installation default for number of sessions, if specified in the configuration file, can be overridden in individual Teradata FastLoad job scripts, when necessary.

BTEQ

The NOTIFY command is provided for use in an operator-free environment, where job scheduling relies heavily on automation to optimize system performance. The function provides hooks that system programmers can use to automate BTEQ job streams fully so they can be integrated with third party vendor products, removing the need to parse the output of BTEQ scripts.

For example, by writing an exit in C (without using CLIv2) and using the NOTIFY...EXIT option, a programmer can provide a means for an automation package to detect that a BTEQ request either succeeds or fails, how many blocks were returned in a successful request, what the return code was for a failed request, and so on.

NOTIFY only applies to the request which immediately follows it.

To get maximum data loading performance, use:

- 5 sessions for each COP or network-attached PE vproc
- 10 sessions for each IFP, depending on the load placed on the AMPs

If the table has secondary indexes, you should probably use a smaller number. If the table is NO FALLBACK, you may require a larger number.

FASTLOAD

If you define a Teradata FastLoad table with a non-unique primary index, you can enhance the performance of the Teradata FastLoad job by *not* using the index value to sort the input data.

Range constraints are data description phrases that you enter in the Teradata SQL CREATE TABLE statement that limit the range of acceptable values for a column. Since the range constraint checks occur while Teradata FastLoad inserts data into the Teradata FastLoad table, the number of range constraints in your Teradata FastLoad job script has a direct impact on the performance of Teradata FastLoad.

FASTEXPORT

Blocksize

FastExport does not automatically block output records. If you want blocked output, you must:

- Specify blocked data (for example, FB) in the record format (RECFM) parameter of the data control block (DCB)
- Specify the block size in the BLOCKSIZE parameter of the DCB

To enhance I/O performance (at the cost of increased storage), increase the value of the network control program (NCP) parameter on an output DCB in your JCL. The maximum value for NCP is 99. The additional storage required is the NCP value multiplied by the block size of the output device.

On VM systems, you may be able to improve the performance of the FastExport utility by specifying RECFM=VBS when:

- The largest row is appreciably smaller than 32K bytes in length
- There is a large variation in row sizes

MULTILOAD

Row vs. field processing

The majority of client processing during a MultiLoad job occurs when it is processing its input rows. The most efficient means of sending the row to the Teradata Database would be a bulk move of the input row to the output row.

However, there are many cases where fields need to be evaluated and field data may need to be individually moved from the input to the output row. Note, however, that performance is affected whenever a field needs to be evaluated or individually moved.

The need for moving individual field data from the input to the output row occurs for any of the following scenarios:

- DROP syntax on FIELD statements
- FILLER fields
- Concatenated fields
- Complex layout (first field is variable-length field, redefinition of field positions)

Variable length fields, NULLIF in the layout, and APPLY WHERE clauses might require additional CPU consumption.

TPUMP

Checklist

The following checklist helps to isolate and analyze TPump performance problems and their causes:

1. Monitor the TPump job using the Monitor macros. Determine whether the job is making progress.
2. Check for locks. The existence of locks can be detected by using the Teradata Database Showlocks utility. The existence of transaction locks can be detected by checking for 'blocked' status Teradata Database utilities that use the performance monitor feature of the Teradata Database.
3. Check table DBC.Resusage for problem areas (for example, data bus capacity or CPU capacity at 100% for one or more processors).
4. Avoid large error tables, if possible, because error processing is generally expensive.

5. Verify that the primary index is unique. Non-unique primary indexes can cause severe TPump performance problems.

Access Logging

Access logging can cause a severe performance penalty. If all successful table updates are logged, a log entry is made for each operation. The primary index of the access logging table may then create the possibility of row hash conflicts.

PPI

You should specify values for the partitioning column set when performing TPump deletes and updates to avoid lock contention problems that can degrade performance. Avoid updating primary index and partitioning columns with TPump to minimize performance degradation.

CPU Usage

Using a large number of NULLIF clauses can cause a significant increase in the CPU usage on the system where you are running TPump. This rise in CPU usage may increase the time the job takes to run.

An increase in CPU usage is most noticeable when you do *not* have:

- FILLER commands in the LAYOUT
- Input position gaps or overlaps
- Concatenated fields
- DROP clauses

To avoid an increase in CPU usage on the system running TPump, transfer the processing of NULLIF expressions to the Teradata Database.

Teradata 14 Solutions Development

TPT

The performance considerations listed above for FastLoad, FastExport, MultiLoad, and TPump also apply to TPT. In addition, the following considerations apply to TPT.

Checkpointing

Checkpointing is a time-consuming operation that impacts performance. To record a checkpoint, Teradata PT must complete the processing of all data in the data streams, log the checkpoint, then go back and continue reading data and writing it to the data streams. In a sense, a job starts and stops at each checkpoint.

Encryption

Encryption may result in a noticeable decrease in load/unload performance due to the time required to encrypt, decrypt, and verify the data, especially when processing very large quantities of data. Take care to encrypt data only when the security benefit is likely to outweigh the performance cost.

Sessions and Instances

Without concrete performance data, no recommendations or guidelines exist for determining the optimum number of sessions or instances. Balancing sessions and instances helps to achieve the best overall job performance without wasting resources.

- Logging on unnecessary sessions is a waste of resources.
- Starting more instances than needed is a waste of resources.

The MaxLoadTask parameter is applied to data transfer operations used by Teradata standalone load and export utilities such as FastLoad, MultiLoad, FastExport, and also Teradata PT, when sending data to or getting data from the Teradata Database. TPump uses normal SQL sessions, and is not affected by this limit.

In Teradata PT, calculating concurrent tasks is different from calculating concurrent tasks in the standalone extract and load utilities. Whereas MultiLoad, FastLoad, and FastExport use one load/unload task per job, a Teradata PT job might use many load/unload tasks per job because a single script can use multiple operators.

Using Default Lengths

Many data types are associated with length specifications *lengthBytes* or *lengthDigits*, which may be either optional or required, depending on datatype. Most of these allow for deferral to the default length value, by simply not specifying the length. However, since the default length is often the maximum length, use of the default value could cause a minor degradation in performance. Be sure to specify length values rather than deferring to the default values when maximizing performance is important.

Parallel Instances

Multiple parallel instances can help improve performance for the Export, Load, and Update operators.

Multi-statement Requests

The most important technique used by the Stream operator to improve performance is the multiple statement request.

SET vs. MULTISET table loading

BTEQ
Since BTEQ uses the standard SQL INSERT command, there are no special considerations.

FASTLOAD
Teradata FastLoad does not load duplicate rows, as in MULTISET tables. If you use Teradata FastLoad to load a target table defined as MULTISET, the utility will discard any duplicate rows. If you must load duplicate rows, consider using MultiLoad.

FASTEXPORT
No special considerations.

MULTILOAD
No special considerations.

TPUMP
No special considerations.

TPT
Same as for the stand-alone utilities, above.

Duplicate Row Elimination

It is not possible to distinguish among duplicate rows in a MULTISET table. Because of this, when a WHERE condition of a DELETE statement identifies a duplicate row, the system deletes all of the identified duplicate rows.

To reduce duplicate rows in a MULTISET table to a single unique row, do an INSERT/SELECT into a SET table. The following table summarizes the restrictions on duplicate rows and INSERT/SELECT:

UTILITIES

FOR this table type...	Duplicate rows are...	
MULTISET with no uniqueness constraints	Permitted. Inserted duplicate rows are stored in the table.	
MULTISET with uniqueness constraints	Not permitted. An error message is returned to the requestor.	
SET	Not permitted.	
	In this session mode...	**The Teradata Database...**
	ANSI	rejects the entire transaction and returns an error message to the requestor.
	Teradata	Rejects the duplicate rows in the transaction. Inserts the non-duplicate rows into the table. Does not return an error message to the requestor.

Figure 7.15

Data availability and integrity

The locks acquired by the various utilities affect the availability of data, and control maintaining data integrity

BTEQ and TPT SQL Inserter

These use the standard SQL locks discussed in Chapter 4.

TPump and TPT Stream

The utility uses conventional row hash locking, which allows for some amount of concurrent read and write access to its target tables. At any point, the utility can be stopped, making the target tables fully accessible. If the utility is stopped, however, depending on the nature of the update process, the relational integrity of the data may be compromised.

Although the utility always uses conventional row hash locking, based on the nature of SQL statements used in the job and the status of the target tables, a job may introduce other levels of locking in a job run. For example, if a target table of a job has a trigger defined and this trigger uses table-level locking when it is triggered, this job may cause a table level-locking if such a trigger is triggered during the run. The script developer should be familiar with the property of the database on which the utility will run and be aware of such possibilities.

The SERIALIZE option can be used to reduce lock contention. Some advantages of the SERIALIZE option are:

- It can eliminate lock delays or potential deadlocks caused by PI collisions from multiple sessions.
- It can also reduce deadlocks when rows with NUPI values are being processed.

FastExport and TPT Export

If you use a LOCKING modifier, the specified lock remains in effect during execution of all statements within the request containing the modifier.
The Teradata Database:

- Implements all resource locks for the entire request before executing any of the statements in the request

UTILITIES

- Maintains the locks until all of the response data for the request has been moved to spool tables
- Removes the resource locks before returning the data to your client system.

FastLoad and TPT Load

When you run a multi-file Teradata FastLoad job, the Teradata FastLoad table and the two error tables remain locked and are not available to users until you use the END LOADING command to conclude the Teradata FastLoad job.

MultiLoad and TPT Update

Acquisition Phase - MultiLoad uses the access lock to allow concurrent select access to all affected target tables throughout the entire import task. Concurrent DML statements that require read or write locks are permitted during the acquisition phase:

- Until MultiLoad finishes acquiring data from the client system
- While conducting a sort of the acquired data

Application Phase – The system upgrades the lock to a Write lock, making the target table available to the users using an Access lock. Concurrent DML statements are not permitted during the application and cleanup phases of an import task.

Once Update execution has started, the target table headers are updated indicating that an Update is in progress. Even if the update doesn't complete successfully, the target tables are still marked as being under control of the utility and access to them will be restricted accordingly.

Load Strategies

The following chart summarizes the utilities that can be used to load data into Teradata Database.

UTILITY	FUNCTION	TARGET TABLE
FastLoad TPT Load	Load large amounts of rows to a single table	Must be empty with no secondary or join indexes
MultiLoad TPT Update	Load, update, delete large number of rows to one or more tables	May be populated. May have non-unique secondary indexes (NUSI) and join indexes (JI)
BTEQ T-Pump TPT Stream	Load, update, delete smaller amounts of rows	May be populated. May have secondary indexes and join indexes

Figure 7.16

Using tools such as Viewpoint, AMPUsage, and ResUsage, determine your various CPU and I/O peak utilization periods.

Since some jobs tend to be CPU-bound and others I/O- bound, it is a good idea to determine which jobs fit into which category. You can determine this by means of AMPUsage data analysis.

Knowing which jobs are CPU-bound and which are I/O-bound enables you to recommended scheduling a CPU-bound job with an I/O bound job so that the resource underutilized by one job can be used more fully by the other.

Once you determine your peak system utilization times, you can recommend that some jobs be moved to other time slots. For example, if peak periods are 9 A.M. to 5 P.M., you might want to schedule batch and load jobs overnight to reserve peak daytime hours for DSS queries or HATP (High Availability Transaction Processing).

Chapter 7: Practice Questions

1. BTEQ has _____.
    a. restart logic
    b. retry logic

2. FastLoad _____ tape support for network attached clients.
    a. has
    b. does not have

3. How can FastLoad commands be entered?
    a. Interactively
    b. Batch
    c. Both ways

4. Which utilities can be used to load duplicate rows into a Multiset table?
    a. BTEQ
    b. FastLoad
    c. MultiLoad
    d. TPump

5. FastExport supports which of the following?
    a. Just INMODs
    b. Just OUTMODs
    c. Both INMODs and OUTMODS
    d. Neither INMODs nor OUTMODS

UTILITIES

6. Each MultiLoad Import task can operate on up to _____ different tables or views.
    a. 3
    b. 4
    c. 5
    d. 6
    e. 7
    f. 8

7. TPump supports which of the following?
    a. Just INMODs
    b. Just OUTMODs
    c. Both INMODs and OUTMODS
    d. Neither INMODs nor OUTMODS

8. What level of locking does TPump use?
    a. Database
    b. Table
    c. Row Hash

9. A TPT Standalone Operator _____.
    a. consumes data from an input stream.
    b. does not send or receive data from other operators.
    c. produces data for an output data stream.

10. Which of the following are not permitted in Secondary Index definitions?
    a. Identity columns
    b. QITS columns
    c. LOB columns

11. If a FastLoad target table has a NUPI, you should do which of the following to enhance performance?
    a. Sort the input data on the NUPI.
    b. Sort the input data on something other than the NUPI.

12. If a DELETE . . . WHERE . . . identifies duplicate rows in a MULTISET table, _____.
    a. the system retains one occurrence and deletes the rest.
    b. the system deletes all of the identified duplicate rows.

13. Attempting to do an INSERT/SELECT from a MULTISET table into a SET table will _____ if there are duplicate rows.
    a. abort
    b. succeed

Chapter Notes

Utilize this space for notes, key points to remember, diagrams, areas of further study, etc.

Chapter 8 - Data Integration and Performance

Certification Objectives

- ✓ Given a scenario, select an effective data integration approach based on application requirements.
- ✓ Given a scenario, select an effective data access approach based on differing application requirements.
- ✓ Contrast the update processes for event driven, active data warehouse, and BI environments, and identify their impact on development choices.
- ✓ Correlate physical design solution development choices with data integration performance.
- ✓ Correlate application solution development choices with data integration performance.
- ✓ Correlate Data integration solution development choices with data access performance.
- ✓ Describe the considerations of Unicode data on the interfaces (e.g., JDBC, ODBC, CLI, etc.).

Before You Begin

You should be familiar with the following terms and concepts.

Terms	Key Concepts
Normalization	Integration benefits
Event Driven	Triggers and Queue tables
Queries	Strategic, Tactical, Ad hoc
Integration	ETL vs. ELT
Locking	SQL and HUT locks
PPI/MLPPI	Loading considerations

Development Choices

The following diagram shows the various solutions that can be supported on Teradata Database.

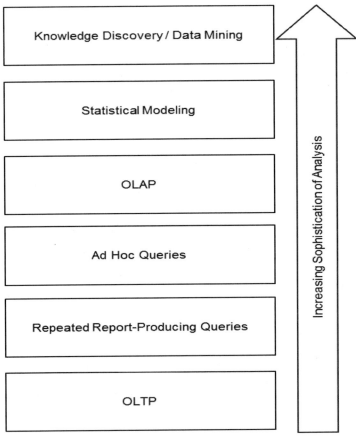

Figure 8.1

Note: Based on the above diagram, as the analysis becomes more complex, the presentation layer to the end user may need to deviate from 3rd normal for optimum performance.

Normalization

Teradata and Normalization

Since its inception, Teradata has promoted fully normalized databases and the Teradata parallel architecture was designed from the outset to support them. Additionally, Normalization has consistently proven to be method for designing logically and provably correct database schemas.

Advantages of Normalization for Physical Database Implementation

The following list summarizes the advantages of physically implementing a normalized logical model for the Teradata Database:

- More primary index choices
- Optimal distribution of data (depending on index selection)
- Fewer full-table scans
- Enhanced likelihood the Optimizer will use the performance merge or nested join methods
- Optimal data separation to eliminate redundancy from the database
- Optimal control of data by eliminating update anomalies
- Optimal application separation
- Optimal control of data
- Optimal data blocking by the file system
- Reduced transient and permanent journal space
- Reduced physical I/O

Design For Decision Support and Tactical Analysis, Not OLTP Applications

Not only is basic schema normalization an important design consideration, but normalization tailored specifically for the analytical needs of business intelligence is also critical. Even fully normalized data warehouses are often built as if they were designed to support OLTP applications.

Designers often fail to examine the following list of considerations:

- Integration of subject areas
- Versioning across time
- Generalization of key entities in anticipation of change
- Interrelation of life cycles across many cross-subject area entities and events
- Integration of measures, calculations, and dimensional context paths across the enterprise

These factors all support the immediate and long-term benefits provided by a fully normalized enterprise data model. The fully normalized schema provides a framework both for continued growth and for increasing user insight.

Note: It is recommended to not use the source OLTP systems for analytics. The preferred approach is to design on an integrated Teradata Data Warehousing for analytics.

Design for Flexible Access Using Views

As a general rule, the best practice is to design applications to access the database *only* through views rather than accessing base tables directly.

DATA INTEGRATION AND PERFORMANCE

Besides providing you with the ability to provide pseudo-denormalized access for enhanced usability, views also provide a degree of data independence that permits you to make changes either to your applications or to the physical database those applications access without having to worry about rewriting application software.

In addition, view projections of the base tables can also reduce the complexity of user queries by creating views that pre-join tables together. This simplifies the query operation and can assist in better performance.

Finally, views can also provide a coarse level of schema versioning that is otherwise not available. Only the application utilities (FastLoad, MultiLoad, TPump, FastExport) should have direct access to the base tables. However, there has been a recent trend where customers have been using the load utilities through base table views and not direct to tables.

Note: You can more readily control locking for access through careful view design. This approach will minimize the complexity of applications that access the database through these views.

Event driven

Queue Tables

A queue table is a persistent database table with the properties of an asynchronous first-in-first-out (FIFO) queue. The queue table is different from a standard base table in that a queue table always contains a user-defined Queue Insertion Timestamp (QITS) as the first column of the table.

The QITS contains the time the row is inserted into the queue table as a way to establish FIFO ordering. Even though the QITS value may not be unique, Teradata Database ensures uniqueness of the ROWID in the queue.

In the past, in order to implement event processing in Teradata Database, customer applications would have had to poll an empty table periodically for inserted rows placed there by another application at an earlier time.

The Queue Table feature provides a non-polling solution that allows information to be made immediately available to database applications instead of their having to wait for a polling interval to complete.

Triggers

The trigger defines events that happen when some other event, called a triggering event, occurs. This database object is essentially a stored SQL statement associated with a table called a *subject* table. Triggers execute when any of the following modifies a specified column or columns in the subject table:

- DELETE
- INSERT
- UPDATE

Typically, the stored SQL statements perform a DELETE, INSERT, or UPDATE on a table different from the subject table.

Business Intelligence (BI)

Business intelligence (BI) mainly refers to computer-based techniques used in identifying, extracting, and analyzing business data, such as sales revenue by products and/or departments, or by associated costs and incomes.

Common functions of business intelligence technologies are reporting, online analytical processing, analytics, data mining, process mining, complex event processing, business performance management, benchmarking, text mining and predictive analytics. The overall goal of Business intelligence is to support better business decision-making.

Ordered Analytical Functions

ANSI Standard Ordered Analytic functions provide the ability to perform aggregations on data and, unlike standard aggregation, retain the detail. For instance, one may not only sum sales amounts of each store by item for all stores and items, but also project additional information such as the store locations, store manager information, vendor names, and even the sales amounts being summed.

These functions fall into 4 classifications of "windowing" capabilities:

- GROUP window (i.e. subtotals)
- CUMULATIVE window (i.e. accumulating totals from "preceding" rows)
- MOVING window (i.e. over a discrete time period size)
- REMAINING window (i.e. accumulating totals from "following" rows)

Ordered analytical functions allow you to perform sophisticated data mining on the information in your databases to get the answers to questions that SQL otherwise cannot provide.

The "EXPLAIN" of these functions appear as "stat functions". In general, these functions allow one to perform sophisticated and creative data mining operations on your data.

Third party tools

Teradata Database supports many third-party software products. The two general components of supported products include those of the transparency series and the native interface products.

Many third-party interactive query products operate in conjunction with Teradata Database, permitting queries formulated in a native query language to access Teradata Database. One major consideration is whether third party vendors from whom you are considering buying tools are Teradata partners. Query tools, for example, should take advantage of the Teradata optimizations (*i.e. they should incorporate the standard Teradata Database aggregate and ordered analytical functions rather than performing in-line calculations of OLAP statistics*).

It is very easy to connect to a Teradata system, whether using a Microsoft Windows, MP-RAS UNIX, Linux, or mainframe system. You can connect to Teradata through a variety of drivers. Teradata has drivers to support ODBC, OLE DB, ADO.NET (Teradata .NET Data Provider), and JDBC. In addition, Teradata has a Call Level Interface (CLI), which allows for robust and tightly integrated application development.

Active Data Warehouse

An active data warehouse:

- Provides a single up-to-date view of the enterprise on one platform.
- Represents a logically consistent store of detailed data available for strategic, tactical, and event driven business decision making.
- Relies on timely updates to the critical data - as close to real time as needed.

DATA INTEGRATION AND PERFORMANCE

- Supports short, tactical queries that return in seconds, alongside of traditional decision support.

Strategic Queries

Strategic queries represent business questions that are intended to draw strategic advantage from large stores of data.

Strategic queries are often complex queries, involving aggregations and joins across multiple tables in the database. They are sometimes long-running and tend not to have a strict service level expectation.

Strategic queries are sometimes ad hoc. They may require significant database resources to execute and they are often submitted from third-party tools.

Tactical Queries

Tactical queries are short, highly tuned queries that facilitate action-taking or decision making in a time-sensitive environment. They usually come with a clear service level expectation and consume a very small percentage of the overall system resources.

Tactical queries are usually repetitively executed and take advantage of techniques such as request (query plan) caching and session-pooling.

As an active data warehouse, Teradata Warehouse provides the following:

- Strategic Intelligence entails delivering intelligence through tools and utilities and query mechanisms that support strategic decision-making. This includes, for example, providing users with simple as well as complex reports throughout the day which indicate the business trends that have occurred and that

are occurring, which show why such trends occurred, and which predict if they will continue to occur.
- Operational Intelligence entails delivering intelligence through tools and utilities and query mechanisms that support front-line or operational decision-making. This includes, for example, ensuring aggressive Service Level Goals (SLGs) with respect to high performance, data freshness, and system availability.
- Active Load is the ability to load data actively and in a non-disruptive manner and, at the same time, process other workloads.
- Active Access provides intelligence for operational and customer interactions consistently.
- Active Events is the ability to detect a business event automatically, apply business rules against current and historical data, and initiate operational actions when appropriate.
- Active Workload Management means the Teradata Warehouse is able to manage mixed workloads dynamically and to optimize system resource utilization to meet business goals.
- Active Enterprise Integration means the Teradata Warehouse is able to integrate itself into enterprise business and technical architectures, especially those that support business users, partners, and customers. This simplifies the task of coordinating enterprise applications and business processes.
- Active Availability means the Teradata Warehouse is able to meet business objectives for its own "uptime". Moreover, it assists customers in identifying application-specific availability, recoverability, and performance requirements based on the impact of enterprise downtime.

Data integration

EXTRACT

Extract in this sense normally refers to extract from the source system for load into the Teradata Database. This would include processes to extract from source systems like Oracle, Golden Gate, MQSeries, flat files, named pipes etc. When bringing data into the Teradata Database, the use of Inmods makes accessing a variety of source inputs possible.

When it comes to extracting data from the Teradata Database, to ship to another Teradata Database, the parallel architecture coupled with FastExport, or TPT Export, reduces the workload for the receiving system.

Note: The ability for the Teradata Data Warehouse to "Multi-thread" exporting data to a client file makes the TPT Export utility a valuable commodity.

LOAD

The various load utilities discussed in a previous chapter allow data to be loaded:

- Stage Loading – TPT Load / FastLoad
- In batch – TPT Update / MultiLoad
- Continuous – TPT Stream / TPump
- Low Volume Data Loads – TPT SQL Inserter / BTEQ

TRANSFORM

Rather than spending CPU cycles transforming data a record at a time, the architecture of the system allows this to be accomplished in parallel through an INSERT/SELECT from a staging table to the target table.

Also, consider the richness of data types and languages supported by the Teradata Database, and UDTs (User-Defined Types) that allow you to create custom data types that model the structure and behavior of data in your applications.

Data access

In an active data warehouse, many people need or want access to the database, for different reasons. Controlling who can do what, to what, and when they can do it, is simplified by the following Teradata Database capabilities:

- Access Rights – The privilege granted to a user to perform specific functions on specific database objects.
- Roles – A way of simplifying the assignment of access rights.
- Profiles – Used to make the management of user settings like accounts, spool space, etc. easier.
- Locking and Transient Journaling – Guarantees that every transaction takes the database from one consistent state to another consistent state, or in the case of a failure, returns the database to its starting consistent state.
- Utility locks – These locks guarantee that users cannot access target tables until the utility has completed its tasks.
- Views – Isolate the base tables from the query users for better control, and provide virtual schemas, well-tuned queries, and controlled access to sensitive data among other things.
- Macros – Frequently used to produce canned reports. The user only has to have EXECute privilege on the macro.
- Stored Procedures - Allow the combination of both SPL (Stored Procedures Language) and SQL. The user only has to have CALL privilege to execute a stored procedure.

Unicode

Unicode is a 16-bit encoding of virtually all characters in all current languages in the world. The UNICODE server character set is designed to eventually store all character data on the server.

Teradata provides text files that define character set mappings and collation sequences for all supported languages. These files can be found on the documentation CD.

Here is a small sampling of the available text files:

File Name on CD	Description
A6A0SUCD.txt	Maps ARABIC1256 to Unicode.
C2A0SUCD.txt	Maps CYRILLIC1251 to Unicode.
EUC2UNCD.txt	Maps KanjiEUC Code Set 2 characters (JISx0201 Katakana) to their Unicode equivalents.
H5A0SUCD.txt	Maps HEBREW1255 to Unicode.
L1A0SUCD.txt	Maps LATIN1250 to Unicode.
S6R0SUCD.txt	Maps SCHINESE936 to Unicode.
T8R0MUCD.txt	Maps the multibyte character portion of TCHINESE950 to Unicode.

Figure 8.2

A Unicode character string literal can consist of a maximum of 31,000 *Unicode* characters.

The data type of Unicode character literals is VARCHAR(n) CHARACTER SET UNICODE, where n is the resolved length of the literal in Unicode characters.

A Unicode character literal is useful for inserting a character string containing characters that cannot generally be entered directly on the terminal keyboard.

Teradata 14 Solutions Development

If your application is intended to be ANSI-compliant and portable, you can replace existing hexadecimal character literals of the form '*hexadecimal digits*'XC with Unicode character literals.

Considerations for Loading PPI and MLPPI Tables

The load and unload utilities can be used with PPI tables.

There are minor restrictions on deletes and updates submitted from MultiLoad or TPump. The historical restriction that values must be supplied for all primary index columns is extended to also require values for all partitioning columns. The historical restriction that primary index columns may not be updated is extended to also disallow updates to the partitioning columns.

Note: Similar restrictions apply to other statements, such as UPSERT or MERGE INTO, for similar reasons.

Bulk inserts and deletes can benefit from partitioning if the partitioning expression is related to the data arrival pattern and data retention policy. This will ordinarily be the case when the partitioning column is the transaction date, and is unlikely to be true otherwise. When the transactions for the current day are processed, the inserted rows will be scattered more or less evenly among all the data blocks of a non-partitioned table.

Continuous TPump updates may benefit to a lesser extent when the table is partitioned on transaction date. The inserted rows will be in a smaller subset of the data blocks, so a data block is somewhat more likely to be in the file system cache when next needed, reducing the number of disk reads. However, a partition with only a few rows in many ways looks like a table with only a few rows, and that can cause serialization of multiple-session TPump (or BTEQ) inserts.

The file system has a locking protocol (not the same locking mechanism which is mentioned in EXPLAIN text) that protects a data block against concurrent inserts or updates from more than one session. When the number of data blocks on an AMP (in a table or in a partition of a table) is small compared to the number of sessions on that AMP, the data block locking protocol has the effect of serializing the multiple sessions. This serialization is most pronounced when all the rows on an AMP fit in one data block, and ceases to be noticeable when the number of data blocks becomes much larger than the number of sessions.

If multiple-session TPump will be used with a PPI table, it may be desirable to define the partitions with fairly coarse granularity, to minimize the number of days per year when the partition corresponding to the current date contains only a few rows. Using a smaller data block size can also reduce the serialization effect, as the number of data blocks will more quickly become large compared to the number of sessions with a smaller data block size. The serialization effect is greatly reduced when this feature is available and activated.

FastExport will generally be affected by the same factors affecting a SELECT statement against a PPI table as discussed earlier. For example, partition elimination can improve the performance of executing the SELECT of the data from a PPI table in a FastExport job.

Considerations for Loading NoPI Tables

The load and unload utilities can be used with NoPI tables. Due to the nature of NoPI table, all loads are generally faster than when loading into PI tables.

Note: TPump can achieve better overall performance with NoPI tables. However, FastLoad is still generally faster when loading either PI or NoPI tables.

Chapter 8: Practice Questions

1. A fully normalized database is good for _____.
    a. OLTP but not data warehousing
    b. data warehousing but not OLTP
    c. all applications

2. Which of the following apply to views?
    a. They can provide pseudo-denormalized access
    b. They can provide schema versioning
    c. They provide better locking control
    d. They can minimize spool on joins
    e. All of the above

3. _____ functions produce a result for each detail item.
    a. Aggregate
    b. Ordered analytic

4. _____ functions do not produce a result for each detail item.
    a. Aggregate
    b. Ordered analytic

5. Which of the following tend to have strict service level expectations?
    a. Strategic queries
    b. Tactical queries

6. Which of the following tend to be long running?
    a. Strategic queries
    b. Tactical queries

Chapter Notes

Utilize this space for notes, key points to remember, diagrams, areas of further study, etc.

Chapter 9 - Maintaining Data Integrity

Certification Objectives

- ✓ Given a scenario with a multi-statement transaction, identify the lock modifier placement options and considerations.
- ✓ Given a CREATE TRIGGER statement, describe which events will take place upon firing the trigger, and in which sequence they will occur.
- ✓ Given a scenario, identify the benefits of using a multi-statement request vs. a multi-statement transaction.
- ✓ Given a scenario, identify the considerations between ANSI and Teradata transactions.
- ✓ Given a scenario, identify the appropriate coding construct (stored procedure, macro, UDF, etc.).
- ✓ Given a set of requirements, identify the data integrity features that should be used.
- ✓ Given a scenario with triggers, RI constraints, or check constraints, identify the sequence of specified events that will take place.
- ✓ Determine the similarities and differences among Standard RI, Batch RI, and Soft RI.

Before You Begin

You should be familiar with the following terms and concepts.

Terms	Key Concepts
Triggers	Statement, row, before, after
Constraints	Referential, Check
Transaction modes	ANSI, Teradata
Transactions	Implicit, Explicit, Multi-statement, Multi-request
UDTs, UDFs, UDMs	Uses and benefits

Triggers

A trigger contains one or more stored SQL statements that are executed, or fired, when some other event, called a triggering event, occurs. Triggers must be associated with an event and cannot be executed independently.

A trigger is associated with a subject table, and is stored as a named database object. Triggers exist in enabled or disabled states; when disabled, triggers remain as inactive database objects.

Typically, triggers execute when an INSERT, UPDATE, or DELETE modifies one or more specified columns in the subject table. The stored statements then perform operations such as INSERT, UPDATE, or DELETE on indicated tables, which may include the subject table.

Types of Triggers

Teradata Database supports two types of triggers.

This type of trigger...	Fires for each...
statement	statement that modifies the subject table.
row	row modified in the subject table.

Figure 9.1

When Do Triggers Fire?

You can specify when triggers fire.

WHEN you specify...	THEN the triggered action...
BEFORE	executes before the completion of the triggering event. As specified in ANSI SQL standard, a BEFORE trigger

MAINTAINING DATA INTEGRITY

WHEN you specify . . .	THEN the triggered action . . .
	cannot have data changing statements in the triggered action.
AFTER	executes after completion of the triggering event. **Note:** To support stored procedures the CALL statement is supported in the body of an AFTER trigger. Both row and statement triggers can call a stored procedure.

Figure 9.2

Sometimes a statement fires a trigger, which in turn, fires another trigger. Thus the outcome of one triggering event can itself become another trigger.

According to ANSI semantics, if the subject table, on which a trigger is defined, is referred anywhere inside a BEFORE trigger or inside an AFTER trigger, then those references would be able to see the rows before or after the operation on the subject table, respectively.

ANSI-Specified Order

When you specify multiple triggers on a subject table, both BEFORE and AFTER triggers execute in the order in which they were created as determined by the timestamp of each trigger.

Triggers are sorted according to the preceding ANSI rule, unless you use Teradata Database extension, ORDER. This extension allows you to specify the order in which the triggers execute, regardless of creation time stamp.

Why Use a Trigger?

You can use triggers to do various things:

- Define a trigger on the subject table to ensure that UPDATEs and DELETEs performed to the subject table are propagated to another table.
- Use triggers for auditing. For example, you can define a trigger which causes INSERTs in a log table when an employee receives a raise higher than 10%.
- Use a trigger to disallow massive UPDATEs, INSERTs, or DELETEs during business hours.
- Use a trigger to set a threshold. For example, you can use triggers to set thresholds for inventory of each item by store, to create a purchase order when the inventory drops below a threshold, or to change a price if the daily volume does not meet expectations.
- Use a trigger to call Teradata Database stored procedures and external stored procedures.

Restrictions on Using Triggers

Restrictions on triggers include the following:

- Utilities such as FastLoad and MultiLoad cannot operate on tables defined with enabled triggers. However, you can bulk load these tables if you disable the triggers. If you disable triggers to use FastLoad and MultiLoad, remember that triggers sometimes define relationships between tables as an extension to Referential Integrity. Therefore, when disabling triggers to use FastLoad and MultiLoad, be careful that relationships maintained with triggers enabled are still maintained by the application using the load utilities.
- You cannot combine row and statement operations within a single trigger definition.

MAINTAINING DATA INTEGRITY

- BEFORE statement triggers are not allowed.
- You cannot define triggers on a table that already has a hash index defined.
- A positioned (updatable cursor) UPDATE or DELETE is not allowed to fire a trigger. An attempt to do so generates an error.
- You cannot use a SET QUERY_BAND statement in a trigger.

RI Constraints

Referential Integrity constraints are created through a REFERENCES clause in a CREATE TABLE statement. They can be specified at the column level, or the table level.

The following restrictions apply:

- If REFERENCES is specified in a *column_constraint*, then *table_name* defines the referenced table. *table_name* must be a non-queue base table, not a view.
- You cannot specify REFERENCES constraints for queue, global temporary, trace, or volatile tables.
- You cannot specify REFERENCES constraints for identity columns.
- A REFERENCES constraint cannot reference UDT, LOB, Period, or Geospatial columns.
- A REFERENCES constraint cannot reference columns in a queue table.
- While it is possible to create a child table at a time that its parent table does not yet exist, a REFERENCES constraint that makes a forward reference to a table that has not yet been created cannot qualify the parent table name with a database name.

In other words, the forward-referenced parent table that has not yet been created must be assumed to be "contained" in the same database as its child table that is currently being created.

The following table describes the basic differences between the different types of referential constraint types:

Referential Constraint Type	DDL Definition Clause	Does It Enforce Referential Integrity?	Level of Referential Integrity Enforcement
Standard RI Constraint	REFERENCES	Yes	Row
Batch Referential Integrity Constraint	REFERENCES WITH CHECK OPTION	Yes	There must be a parent table row for all child rows.
Soft Referential Constraint	REFERENCES WITH NO CHECK OPTION	No	None
Temporal Relationship Constraint	REFERENCES WITH NO CHECK OPTION	No	None

Figure 9.3

The different types of referential constraints have different applications:

Referential Constraint Type	Application
Standard Referential Integrity constraint	• Before each individual insertion, deletion, or update the database tests each row for referential integrity.

MAINTAINING DATA INTEGRITY

Referential Constraint Type	Application
	- AMP software will reject any operation and return an error message if the insertion, deletion, or update of a row would violate referential integrity - Special optimization is permitted for certain queries. - This type of constraint is not valid for temporal tables
Batch Referential Integrity constraint	- An entire insert, delete, or update request operation is tested for referential integrity. (In this context, a batch operation is defined as an implicit SQL transaction.) - The request is aborted and the system returns an error to the requestor if the result of the request violates referential integrity. - Special optimization is permitted for certain queries. - This type of constraint is not valid for temporal tables.
Soft Referential constraint	- No implicit tests for referential integrity. - It is assumed that the user has somehow enforced referential integrity via application development. - Special optimization is permitted for certain queries. - This type of constraint is valid for both temporal tables and nontemporal tables.
Temporal Relationship Constraint	- No implicit tests for referential integrity.

Referential Constraint Type	Application
	- It is assumed that the user has somehow enforced referential integrity via application development. - Special optimization is permitted for certain queries. - You can only define Temporal Relationship Constraints at the table level.

Figure 9.4

Standard

Standard referential integrity checks the equality row by row, ensuring data integrity during insert, delete, or update operations on a table. However, this fine granularity incurs a modest performance overhead.

Note: Foreign key references are not allowed in MultiLoad or FastLoad target tables.

Batch

A batch referential integrity constraint is less expensive to enforce than standard referential integrity because checking is performed on qualified rows within a transaction rather than on all rows in the table.

When the reference point is reached, the parser joins the Parent and Child rows and then tests them. If a violation is found, all statements in the transaction are rolled back. Thus, the enhanced performance can incur the following costs:

MAINTAINING DATA INTEGRITY

- With very large tables, a rollback can be expensive. You should use Batch RI only for smaller tables, or those whose normal workloads will not trigger reference violations.
- Query results might be inaccurate, depending on the type and amount of operations in the transaction and how deeply into the transaction the first violation is detected.
- Utilities like FastLoad and MultiLoad are not able to operate on tables defined for batch referential integrity checking.

Soft

No constraints are enforced when you use the WITH NO CHECK OPTION with the REFERENCES clause in the CREATE TABLE or ALTER TABLE statement. Referential Constraint does not incur the overhead of the database-enforced referential integrity.

Note: Soft RI is definitely encouraged and recommended on Teradata over the other methods discussed.

Temporal

Temporal Referential Constraints define relationships where every time based value (date, time, timestamp) in a column of a child table exists within a time period stored within a column of a parent table. These constraints are "soft" because Teradata does not enforce them. Additionally, they can be utilized by the Optimizer to improve query performance by eliminating redundant joins even though they are not enforced.

Check Constraints

Check constraints are used to ensure that data in certain fields meet a predefined criteria. They are applied during insertion or an update. For example, if there is field called GENDER on a table, a Check constraint can be defined to ensure that only the values 'M', 'F', or

NULL are present. When a Check constraint is violated, an error is reported.

Note: The current session collation for character data is what is used to check the values. This means that, while rare, it is possible for a Check constraint to allow a value during one session but not for another session if the collation has changed.

Transaction mode

Teradata performs transaction processing in either of the following modes:

- ANSI
- Teradata

In ANSI mode, transaction processing adheres to the rules defined by the ANSI SQL specification. In Teradata mode, transaction processing follows the rules defined by Teradata. Below are a few comparisons between the two modes.

TERADATA Mode	ANSI Mode
Data comparison is **not case specific**. Character literal values can be coded in SQL as lower case or upper case. The search engine would view an 'A' the same as an 'a' and data would be returned.	Data comparison is **case specific**. Character literal values must be coded using the correct case in order for the search engine to determine a match. An 'A' is different than an 'a' and data would not be returned.
Allows truncation of displayed data. Certain SQL commands covered in earlier chapters allow the user to request less characters be returned than the	**Forbids truncation** of display data. Any attempt to return less than all the data stored in a column will cause the SQL to fail with an error (3996).

MAINTAINING DATA INTEGRITY

TERADATA Mode	ANSI Mode
number of characters stored in a column. This is perfectly acceptable.	
A transaction is **implicit** by nature – each SQL statement is a stand-alone transaction and the work committed upon a successful completion. A transaction can also be **explicit** with a BEGIN TRANSACTION (BT) command and an END TRANSACTION (ET) command. The presence of the ET command will cause all successfully completed SQL work to be committed and make it permanent.	All transactions are **explicit only** and at the end of a transaction a COMMIT WORK command is required in order to commit all successfully completed work and make it permanent.
The **CREATE TABLE** will default to: • **SET** table (no duplicate rows allowed). • Non-case specific character data columns.	The **CREATE TABLE** will default to: • MULTISET table (duplicate rows allowed). • Case specific character data columns.

Figure 9.5

The ACID Properties of Transactions

The general concept of transaction processing is encapsulated by their so-called ACID properties. ACID is an acronym for the following set of properties that characterize any correct database transaction:

- Atomicity
- Consistency
- Isolation

- Durability

The specific meanings of these expressions in terms of database transactions are defined in the following table:

TERM	DEFINITION
Atomicity	A transaction either occurs or it does not. No matter how many component SQL operations are specified within the boundaries of a transaction, they must all complete successfully and commit or they must all fail and rollback. There are no partial transactions.
Consistency	A transaction transforms one consistent database state into another. Intermediate inconsistencies in the database are not permitted.
Isolation	The operations of any transaction are concealed from all other transactions until that transaction commits. Isolation is a synonym for serializable.
Durability	Once a commit has been made, the new consistent state of the database survives even if the underlying system crashes. Durability is a synonym for persistent.

Figure 9.6

It should be clear that the degree of shared variance among them varies considerably. For example, Atomicity and Consistency are very close to being subtle restatements of one another, and neither is possible without Isolation.

Furthermore, the importance of the various ACID guarantees will depend on whether a transaction is read-only or if it also performs write operations. In the case of a read-only transaction, for example, Atomicity and Durability are irrelevant, but Isolation remains critically important.

MAINTAINING DATA INTEGRITY

Note that transactions are not always atomic in ANSI mode because when a request within a transaction fails with an Error response, only that request, not the entire transaction, is rolled back. The remainder of the transaction continues until it either commits or rolls back.

To ensure that your ANSI transactions are always handled as intended, it is critical to code your applications with logic to handle any situations that only roll back an error-generating request rather than the entire transaction of which it is a member.

In ANSI mode, transactions are always *explicit*. Each ANSI transaction is *implicitly* initiated, but always *explicitly* completed.

A transaction begins with the first request submitted in a session and continues until the system encounters either an explicit COMMIT statement or an explicit ROLLBACK statement, at which point it ends, releasing all the locks it held, discarding the Transient Journal, and closing any open cursors.

Teradata

Transactions can be implicit or explicit. Unless bounded by explicit BEGIN TRANSACTION (BT) and END TRANSACTION (ET) statements, the system treats each request as an implicit transaction.

Explicit transaction boundaries are specified using BEGIN TRANSACTION (BT) and END TRANSACTION (ET). BTET means that you can optionally code transaction initiation and termination explicitly in Teradata session mode, but not in ANSI session mode. In ANSI session mode, all transactions begin implicitly, but must be terminated explicitly.

When a transaction fails, the system first rolls it back automatically, discards its Transient Journal, releases all locks, and closes any open cursors. Statement Failure responses roll back the entire transaction, not just the request that evokes them.

In creating a User, the system administrator decides whether the default transaction processing mode will conform to the ANSI standards, or the Teradata standards. The following chart reviews the comparison differences.

IF transaction semantics are...	Then the default for comparisons is...
ANSI	CASESPECIFIC
Teradata	NOT CASESPECIFIC

Figure 9.7

Setting the Transaction Mode

The default mode in Teradata is Teradata mode which is set at the system level. To set the transaction processing mode, use the:

- SessionMode field of the DBS Control Record
- Preprocessor2 TRANSACT() option
- BTEQ command .SET SESSION TRANSACTION (shown below)

```
-- set transaction mode to Teradata
.SET SESSION TRANSACTION BTET;
```

Figure 9.8

or

```
-- set transaction mode to ANSI
.SET SESSION TRANSACTION ANSI;
```

Figure 9.9

Multi-statement requests

Here are some terms associated with transaction processing that you should understand:

TERM	DEFINITION
Statement	A SQL command that ends with a semicolon.
Request	One or more statements sent to the Parser for execution.
Transaction	One or more requests that take the database from one consistent state to another consistent state.

Figure 9.10

Implicit Transactions

BTEQ accepts SQL input until it reaches a line that ends with a semicolon as the last non-blank character. It then sends what it has read to the Parser for processing. The input may consist of one or more SQL statements. Whatever is sent is considered a transaction.

The following example illustrates three single-statement requests and one multi-statement request:

```
-- Txn1
INSERT INTO . . . ;
-- Txn 2
UPDATE t1 SET . . . ;
-- Txn 3
DELETE FROM . . . ;
-- Txn 4
INSERT INTO . . .
; UPDATE t2 SET . . .
; DELETE FROM . . . ;
```

Figure 9.11

In the above example, each request is also treated as a transaction.

Another example of creating a multi-statement request, that is also a single transaction, is a Macro. A macro always represents a single transaction, regardless of how many SQL statements it contains. Macros contain an implicit BT;. . . ET;

```
CREATE MACRO single_transaction AS
(SELECT . . . ;
 SELECT . . . ;
 INSERT INTO . . . ;
 UPDATE . . . ;
 DELETE . . . ;
 MERGE INTO . . . ;
);
```

Figure 9.12

Multi-request Transactions

TRANSACTION SEMANTICS – BTET MODE

Implicit transaction

- Each SQL request is an implicit transaction by default.
- Each failed request is automatically rolled back.

Explicit transaction

- Launched with explicit BEGIN TRANSACTION (BT)

MAINTAINING DATA INTEGRITY

Ended explicitly by:

- END TRANSACTION (ET)—commit work done since BT
- ROLLBACK—rollback work done since BT

Ended implicitly by:

- Any request failure—rollback work done since BT

Examples:

Implicit Transaction	Explicit Transaction
.LOGON INSERT row1; (txn#1) INSERT row2; (txn#2) .LOGOFF	BT; (txn#1) INSERT row1; INSERT row2; ET;
Two requests. Two transactions. Failure of one doesn't affect the other.	Two requests. One transaction. Failure of one will rollback to BT.

Figure 9.13

ANSI Mode Transactions

Apart from transaction semantics, you can write SQL code with explicit specifications to override defaults so that it performs identically in both ANSI and Teradata modes. The following rules are enforced in ANSI mode.

A transaction initiation is always *implicit*. A transaction is opened by the first SQL statement executed in a session or by the first statement executed following the close of a transaction. The COMMIT [WORK] or ROLLBACK [WORK] statements close a transaction.

In ANSI mode, the user must commit the work to disk in order to save the work. The COMMIT WORK; command must be used to successfully end an ANSI transaction (single or multi-step command).

TRANSACTION SEMANTICS – ANSI MODE

Explicit transaction

- Transaction is launched with first SQL request.
- All transactions are explicitly ended.
- Transaction ended explicitly by:
    - COMMIT WORK—commit work done since launch
    - ROLLBACK—rollback work done since launch

Examples:

No Explicit Ending	**Explicit Ending**
.LOGON INSERT row1; (txn#1) INSERT row2; .LOGOFF	.LOGON INSERT row1; (txn#1) INSERT row2; COMMIT WORK; .LOGOFF
Two requests. One transaction. LOGOFF without COMMIT – both INSERTs roll back.	Two requests. One transaction. Failure of either has no effect on the other. COMMIT commits successful requests only.

Figure 9.14

MAINTAINING DATA INTEGRITY

ANSI vs. BTET

The following chart illustrates the differences between ANSI, Explicit, and Implicit transactions:

ANSI mode	BTET mode – Explicit	BTET mode – Implicit

UPD A
UPD B
COMMIT
/* both commit */
	BT
	  UPD A
	  UPD B
	ET
	/* both commit */
		UPD A
		/* A commits */
		UPD B
		/* B commits */

UPD A
UPD B
/* fails */
COMMIT
/* A commits */
	BT
	  UPD A
	  UPD B
	  /* fails */
	/* both rollback */
		UPD A
		/* A commits */
		UPD B
		/* fails */
		/* B rolls back */

UPD A
UPD B
ROLLBACK
/* both rollback */
	BT
	  UPD A
	  UPD B
	LOGOFF
	/* both rollback */
		ROLLBACK is not applicable in implicit transactions.

UPD A
UPD B
LOGOFF
/* both rollback */
	BT
	  UPD A
	  UPD B
	LOGOFF
	/* both rollback */
		UPD A
		/* A commits */
		UPD B
		/* B commits */
		LOGOFF

Figure 9.15

User Defined Functions (UDFs)

You can create User-Defined Functions (UDFs) to address your particular data needs and to fill the void where system-provided SQL functions are lacking. These special functions can translate into time-saving measures by preprocessing data, or by optimizing query processing. Additionally, UDFs can be defined using just regular SQL expressions, called SQL UDFs, or they can be External UDFs that are written in programming languages such as C, C++, or Java.

You can use UDFs to map and manipulate non-text data, such as images, in a way that is impossible with SQL constructs.

Teradata Database supports three types of external UDFs:

- Scalar
- Aggregate
- Table

Scalar Functions

Scalar functions take input arguments and return a single value result. Some examples of standard SQL scalar functions are CHARACTER_LENGTH, ABS, and SQRT.

You can use a scalar function in place of a column name in an expression. When Teradata Database evaluates the expression, it invokes the scalar function. No context is retained after the function completes.

You can also use a scalar function to implement user-defined type (UDT) functionality such as cast, transform, or ordering.

Aggregate Functions

Aggregate functions produce summary results. They differ from scalar functions in that they take grouped sets of relational data, and return one result for the group after making a pass over each group. Some examples of standard SQL aggregate functions are AVG, SUM, MAX, and MIN.

Teradata Database invokes an aggregate function once for each item in the group, passing the detail values of a group through the input arguments. To accumulate summary information, an aggregate function must retain the context each time it is called.

Table Functions

A table function is invoked in the FROM clause of an SQL SELECT statement. It then returns a table one row at a time in a loop to the SELECT statement. The function can produce the rows of a table from the input arguments that are passed to it or by reading a message queue or external file.

The number of columns in the rows that a table function returns can be specified dynamically at runtime in the SELECT statement that invokes the table function.

User-Defined Methods (UDM)

A user-defined method (UDM) is a UDF that is associated with a user-defined type (UDT). Basically, a method as a specialized function that is associated with a UDT and is automatically invoked when the UDT is displayed or changed. Therefore, Methods control how data in a UDT is displayed to the end user, as well as how it is initialized / updated by an application.. Teradata Database supports two types of UDMs:

- **Instance** – Used to initialize or update the UDT value
- **Constructor** – Used to display or export the UDT value

User Defined Type (UDT)

UDTs are custom data types that are defined by the CREATE TYPE statement and allow you to model the structure and behavior of data that your application deals with.

Teradata Database supports two types of UDTs: *distinct* types and *structured* types. A distinct type is based on a single predefined data type such as INTEGER or CHAR. A structured type consists of one or more attributes that are defined as predefined data types or other UDTs.

You can use distinct and structured UDTs as scalar UDF arguments and return values.

Note: UDFs, UDTs, and UDMs can all be stored in the Teradata Data Warehouse.

Chapter 9: Practice Questions

1. Which load utilities can run with triggers enabled?
    a. BTEQ
    b. FastLoad
    c. MultiLoad
    d. TPUMP

2. The ANSI standard states that when you specify multiple triggers on a subject table, both BEFORE and AFTER triggers execute in _____.
    a. BEFORE then AFTER sequence
    b. AFTER then BEFORE sequence
    c. alphabetical sequence
    d. creation timestamp sequence

3. REFERENCES WITH CHECK OPTION defines:
    a. A standard RI constraint.
    b. A batch RI constraint.
    c. A soft Referential constraint.

4. Which of the following apply to Soft Referential Constraints?
    a. Tests each individual inserted, deleted, or updated row for referential integrity.
    b. Tests an entire insert, delete, or update request operation for referential integrity.
    c. Does not check for referential integrity.
    d. Permits special optimization of certain queries.

Teradata 14 Solutions Development

5. On which of the following can a CHECK constraint be applied?
    a. UDT column
    b. BLOB column
    c. CLOB column
    d. Identity column
    e. All of the above
    f. None of the above

6. Which of the following are true if you are in Teradata mode?
    a. Data comparisons are not case specific
    b. Data comparisons are case specific
    c. Truncation of displayed data is allowed
    d. Truncation of displayed data is forbidden
    e. Transactions may be implicit or explicit
    f. Transactions are only explicit
    g. The CREATE TABLE default is SET
    h. The CREATE TABLE default is MULTISET

7. Which of the following are true if you are in ANSI mode?
    a. Data comparisons are not case specific
    b. Data comparisons are case specific
    c. Truncation of displayed data is allowed
    d. Truncation of displayed data is forbidden
    e. Transactions may be implicit or explicit
    f. Transactions are only explicit
    g. The CREATE TABLE default is SET
    h. The CREATE TABLE default is MULTISET

8. BTEQ _____ recognize and handle BT/ET statements.
    a. does
    b. does not

9. Teradata supports _____ UDFs.
    a. Database, table, and row
    b. Aggregate, table, and row
    c. Aggregate, scalar, and table
    d. Scalar, aggregate, and row

10. A ____ is a special kind of ____ that is associated with a ____.
    a. UDF – UDM – UDT
    b. UDF – UDT - UDM
    c. UDM – UDF - UDT
    d. UDM – UDT – UDF
    e. UDT – UDF – UDM

Chapter Notes

Utilize this space for notes, key points to remember, diagrams, areas of further study, etc.

Chapter 10 - Performance Monitoring Tools & Facilities

Certification Objectives

- ✓ Given a scenario, identify the tools that should be used to support performance analysis during the development and test phases.
- ✓ Identify resources available to analyze solution performance metrics that can also be used during testing.

Before You Begin

You should be familiar with the following terms and concepts.

Terms	Key Concepts
Logging	Access Logging, DBQL, Locking Logger
TASM	Tools and uses
Performance Monitoring	PMON, AMPUsage, ResUsage

Access Logging

How Access Logging Works

Each time a user named in a BEGIN LOGGING statement attempts to perform a specified action against a specified object, an entry is logged in the system table *DBC.AccLogTbl*. Possible entry data includes the type of access, the text of the request, the frequency of access, the action requested, the name of the requesting user, and the referenced objects.

Logging can be ended on any action, user, or object for which logging is currently active through the END LOGGING statement. A logging entry does not indicate that a statement was performed; rather, it indicates that the system checked the privileges necessary to perform the statement.

Access Logging on Hash and Join Indexes

Because neither hash indexes nor join indexes can be accessed directly, you cannot specify access logging for either type of object. If you need to perform access logging, specify it for the relevant base table. When a hash or join index is used in a query plan, the access privileges are checked for the base table and logged appropriately.

Setting up Access Logging

To enable logging of access checks, the DBC.AccLogRule macro must exist and you must have EXECUTE privilege on it. The DBC.AccLogRule macro is an empty macro used only for the privilege check.

You activate access checking by defining the rules in one or more BEGIN LOGGING statements. The rules you specify are stored in system table DBC.AccLogRuleTbl. The GRANT options are the same as for the SQL GRANT statement.

The END LOGGING statement erases only the frequency or text flags for the specified actions and user or object. However, if erasing a frequency leaves all logging blank for a particular user, database, and table, then the row is deleted from the *AccLogRuleTbl* table.

PERFORMANCE MONITORING TOOLS & FACILITIES

You must disable access logging to perform an INITIATE INDEX ANALYSIS or RESTART INDEX ANALYSIS statement. Once the index analysis completes, you can enable access logging once again.

Teradata Administrator – Access Logging

Among the many things that the Teradata Administrator utility provides through a window interface is the ability to manage both Access Logging and Query Logging.

From the main window, click **Tools>Access Logging** or click **Tools>Query Logging**.

Database Query Log (DBQL)

Concepts

The Database Query Log (DBQL) is an optional feature that you can employ to log query processing activity for later analysis. Query counts and response times can be charted and SQL text and processing steps can be compared to fine-tune your applications for optimum performance.

DBQL collects information based on rules you specify and flushes the DBQL cache as defined by the DBQLFlushRate field in the DBSControl record every 10 minutes (default) and writes to the DBQL dictionary tables (which are a series of predefined tables also referred to as logs). This information includes historical records of queries and their duration, performance data, and target activity.

DBQL is controlled by the Teradata SQL statements BEGIN QUERY LOGGING and END QUERY LOGGING. Only a user with EXECUTE privilege on DBC.DBQLAccessMacro can invoke the statements.

You cannot issue a BEGIN/END QUERY LOGGING statement while running in ANSI session mode. In Teradata session mode, you cannot issue a BEGIN/END QUERY LOGGING statement within a BT/ET transaction. Instead, use these statements outside a BT/ET transaction or, for ANSI session mode, log off and set the transaction mode to Teradata session mode.

DBC.LogOnOff View

Many of the columns DBQL captures about users logging on and logging off are also available through the DBC.LogOnOff view.

Teradata Query Scheduler

Teradata QS consists of client and server system components that provides a database request scheduling service. Essentially, Teradata QS is a back-end process that accepts new requests, executes scheduled requests, and returns request and status information to the clients at specified times. Therefore, Teradata QS can schedule queries through either the Request Viewer or Teradata SQL Assistant.

Scheduled requests are SQL queries submitted to a Teradata Database that become scheduled for off-line execution. You can schedule requests in two ways:

- Using the **Teradata Query Scheduler Submit Request** dialog box
- Using Teradata SQL Assistant

When you know of existing database rules that will prevent your SQL request from running or if you suspect that your queries will overload your database, you can proactively schedule your request using the **Teradata Query Scheduler Submit Request** dialog box.

PERFORMANCE MONITORING TOOLS & FACILITIES

When you schedule a request, you provide information that defines preferences for when it is executed. You can schedule a request to run periodically or only once during a specified time period without an active user connection to the Teradata Database.

However, scheduling a request does not guarantee that it is executed at the date and time you specify. Your scheduled requests are subject to the same Teradata Database workload management rule checking as are interactive requests.

Teradata Active System Management (TASM)

Teradata Active System Management (TASM) is a suite of products, which includes system tables and logs that are integrated and automated into a centralized data source. TASM combines four key areas of system management:

- Workload Management
- Performance Tuning
- Capacity Planning
- Performance Monitoring

TASM helps manage the system automatically and reduces the effort required by DBAs, application developers, and support personnel. TASM can improve and optimize your workload management and performance. In addition, with careful planning, it can also improve response times and ensure more consistent response times for critical work. The tools comprising TASM are as follows, and will be discussed in order:

- Teradata Viewpoint
- Teradata Workload Analyzer
- Priority Scheduler (PSF)
- Teradata Analyst Pack

- Visual Explain
- Statistics Wizard
- Index Wizard
- Teradata System Emulation Tool (TSET)

Teradata Viewpoint

Teradata Viewpoint is a very useful tool for monitoring and managing Teradata Database systems. Using standard internet browsers, it can be used by both business users and technical users such as database and system administrators.

The information provided by Teradata Viewpoint can help alleviate the workload of DBA's and system admins by reducing the number of status requests they receive from business users. It also allows the administrators to better identify trouble queries or batch jobs as well as trends providing for better planning of system resource usage.

Portlets are the foundation by which Teradata Viewpoint disseminates information to its various users. Preconfigured portlets allow for viewing of system health, query progress, saturation, etc. Access to different portlets can be granted via Roles. Additionally, users can customize the portlets, for which they have access, to suit their needs.

There are four main components of Teradata Viewpoint:

- Viewpoint Server – This is the hardware component that is installed in the Teradata rack and connected via Ethernet.
- Data Collection Service – A Java process that collects daily activities and stores it in a local cache database. The data is used for reporting purposes and can be accessed during system outages due to the data being stored locally and not within Teradata itself.

PERFORMANCE MONITORING TOOLS & FACILITIES

- Viewpoint Portal – This is the foundation for delivering the Viewpoint portlets. It is Java-based and lives on the Viewpoint server.
- Portlets – The preconfigured content that provides the historical view of system usage and capacity as well as the current view of throughput and workload. Many different portlets are available such as System Health, Space Usage, BAR Operations, Workload Designer, My Queries, Alert Viewer, etc.

Teradata Workload Analyzer

The workload analysis process consists of the following steps:

1. The user may optionally migrate existing priority scheduler definitions (PDSets created in PSA), to automatically create workload definitions with the same priority scheduler settings as currently exist. If users choose not to migrate existing settings, they can instead choose to be guided to define workload definitions from scratch. In doing so, users first collect query log information for the existing workload mix. Then they specify the dimensions to analyze and group queries against to form candidate workloads (account-based, application-based, and existing PDSets) and the date and time range to analyze for analysis of the previously collected query log data.
2. Using this input, Teradata WA recommends candidate workload definitions based on analysis of Priority Scheduler Facility settings and/or Database Query Log data.
3. With the DBQL analysis path, the user can further refine the candidate workload definition and the queries in which it contains by either merging with another candidate workload or splitting the candidate workload into two or more separate candidate workloads to aid with accounting granularity or workload control. For example, tactical queries need higher

priority and therefore should be split out from the "parent" candidate workload. Next, users creating workload definitions from scratch (not for users migrating from existing PSF settings) are guided through mapping workload definitions to PSF allocation groups and allocation group weights. Those settings are guided to minimize necessary DBA involvement, though the DBA has the "advanced" option to refine those settings according to the administrator's preference.

4. After the user has satisfactorily fine-tuned the candidate workload definition, the user sets service-level goals, optionally guided by Teradata WA. For example, the user might request recommendations based on actual response times achieved at a particular service-level percent, or other factors.

Priority Scheduler

The information below only applies to Teradata Database systems running on SUSE Linux Enterprise Server (SLES 10). Priority Scheduler is managed by Teradata Active System Management (ASM) and configured, as well as monitored, by Teradata Viewpoint portlets on SUSE Linux Enterprise Server 11 (SLES 11) systems.

Priority Scheduler enables you to do the following:

- Balance resource usage across different applications and utilities
- Authorize users for access to prioritized levels of service based on the PG, carried in the user account string
- Dynamically alter the PG of a user or (with profiles) user group
- Regulate access to AMP worker tasks (AWTs)
- Dynamically modify parameters that define your scheduling strategy, plus:
    - Record these parameters as profiles

- o   Automatically change the profiles at scheduled times
- Set CPU usage limits at a variety of levels

When defining your scheduling strategy, the following parameters are available:

- A prioritized weighting system
- Methods for dynamically adjusting your strategy based on resource use or calendar schedule.

These capabilities allow you to control your workload flow.

Priority Scheduler Architecture

Priority Scheduler consists of Resource Partitions, Resource Groups, and Allocation Groups, as shown in the following diagram.

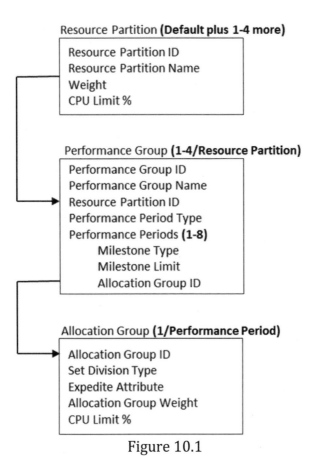

Figure 10.1

Priority Scheduler with TDWM Workloads

If you have been using Priority Scheduler Administrator to manage resource utilization by database requests, Priority Definition (PD) sets are stored on your system. You can transfer these PD sets from Priority Scheduler Administrator and convert them to WD Sets for use with Teradata DWM.

A Workload Definition (WD) is a workload grouping and its operating rules assist in managing queries. The requests that belong to the same workload will share the same resource priority and exception conditions. These conditions consist of the following:

- Classification Criteria: Criteria to determine which queries belong to the workload. This criteria defines characteristics which are detectable prior to query execution. This is also known as the *"who"*, *"where"*, and *"what"* criteria of a query. For example, *"who"* may be an account name, *"where"* is the database tables being accessed, and *"what"* may be the type of statement (INSERT) being executed.

- Exception Criteria: Criteria to specify "abnormal" behavior for queries in this workload. This criterion is only detectable after a query has begun execution. If an exception criteria is met, the request is subject to the specified exception action which may be to lower the priority or abort the query.

- Operating Periods: A description of hours of the day and/or days of the week (or month). Directives may be specified for exception handling and Priority Scheduler settings can be changed for each operating period.

The maximum workloads are 250, with 5 system workloads, leaving 245 available for user defined workloads, each with its own criteria for:

- Queries to include (classify)
- Throttle (concurrency) limit to use
- Priority Scheduler priority to use
- Run-time exception directives
- Service Level Goals (SLGs)

Workload Designer

Workload Designer is a Teradata Viewpoint portlet that helps you with workload management by allowing the creation of rulesets. The following features are available for managing workloads:
- Limits for sessions, which can include query sessions limits, utility limits, and utility sessions limits
- Filters for rejecting certain queries
- Throttles for limiting queries
- Combining environmental status and health status gives you certain States
- Collections of Filters, Throttles, States, workload rules and events. These collections are called Rulesets
- Exceptions that cause defined actions when specific events occur

Workload Health

Workload Health is a Teradata Viewpoint portlet for displaying workload management in a Teradata database. It is your choice as to which system, metrics and workloads to monitor. You can then customize the information that is displayed via Sorting and Filtering menus. The Workload Health portlet is refreshed every 60 seconds and displays:

- Workloads that are inactive
- Disabled workloads
- Workloads that have either missed or met their response time Service Level Goals
- Workloads with no defined response time Service Level Goal

Workloads are groups of queries where a set of defined workload management controls have been applied because they share certain characteristics.

Service Level Goals are defined for reporting and logging purposes and are used for measuring whether queries are meeting defined workload management criteria.

Resource Partitions and Performance Groups

WHAT IS A WEIGHT?

Every Teradata Database logon session is assigned to a Performance Group. Performance Groups control the prioritization of jobs started by sessions under their control. When a Performance Group is defined, it is assigned to a Resource Partition.

Weights are assigned at the Resource Partition level and to Allocation Groups within a Resource Partition. Weights are used at these levels to determine the relative proportion of resources to allocate to the user. Basically, weights are:

- A numeric value used at the Resource Partition Level to compute a relative weight (compared to other Resource Partitions) to determine the proportion of resources the processes of the entire Resource Partition are to receive.

- A numeric value used at the Allocation Group Level to compute a relative weight (within the Resource Partition) to determine the proportion of resources the processes of the Allocation Group is to receive.

Allocation Groups are also associated with Performance Groups. Like Resource Partitions, Allocation Groups have weights that determine the proportion of resources allocated relative to the other Allocation Groups that are active within the same Resource Partition.

EXAMPLE OF PRIORITY WEIGHTS

Let's assume there are four defined Resource Partitions, with individual weight assignments of R1 = 10, R2 = 20, R3 = 40, and R4 = 80. These weights mean nothing to Priority Scheduler unless more than one Resource Partition is active. If there are multiple active Resource Partitions, the weights are used to determine how much of the system's resources a given partition will receive compared to the other active partitions. The formula is very straight forward: Divide the weight of the active partition being measured by the sum of the weights of all of the active partitions. As an example, if R1 and R2 are active, their combined weights add up to 30. The means the R1 will receive 10/30 (.33, or 33%) of the system's resources, and R2 will receive 20/30 (.66 or 66%) of the system's resources. If partitions R2, R3, and R4 are active, the sum of their weights is 140. That means that the system's resource will be distributed across the three active partitions as R2 = 14% (20/140), R3 = 28% (40/140), and R4 = 57% (80/140). If only one Resource Partition is active, it gets 100% of the system's resources.

This same process is used to determine the percentage of resources Allocation Groups within a Resource Group can use. Let's assume the three Allocation Groups under R4, have assigned weights of U1 = 30, U2 = 60, and U3 = 90. If all of them are active, the amount of resources available to R4 will be distributed as U1 = 16% (30/180), U2 = 33% (60/180), and U3 = 50% (90/180).

When a user logs on, a PG's can be specified in the Account String during logon time, but it is not required. PGs do not link RPs and AGs. Queries will be assigned to a PG, either through specifying it in the account string, the default PG or the Milestone. The AG of the query step will be assigned to is based on the Performance Period(s) defined.

PERFORMANCE MONITORING TOOLS & FACILITIES

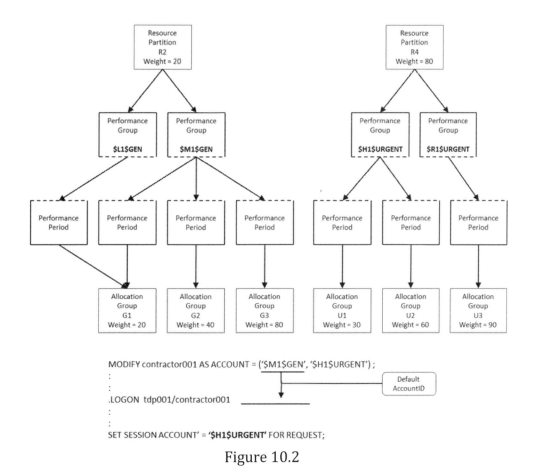

Figure 10.2

Referring to the example illustrated in Figure 7.2, only Resource Partitions R2 and R4 are active at the moment, and the Allocation Groups shown are active. When *contractor001* logged on, the default AccountID put the user in Performance group $M1$GEN. Presently, R2 can use 20% of the system's resources, and R4 can use 80%. Since all three Allocation Groups are active, G1 can use 14% of R2's 20%, G2 can use 28%, and G3 can use 57%. To determine the relative weight of a Performance Group (what percentage of the total system's resources a Performance Group can use), the system simply has to multiply the Resource Partition's active weight against the Allocation Group' active weight. The rules defined for the individual

Performance Groups will determine which Allocation Group will service *contractor001*'s requests. Based upon parameters, like time-of-day, contractor001's requests may dynamically switch Allocation Groups. Assuming that all three Allocation Groups remain active, here are the relative Performance Group weights for $M1$GEN depending upon which Allocation Group is used.

$$G1 = 20/(20+80) * 20/(20+40+80) = .2 * .14 = 2\%$$
$$G2 = 20/(20+80) * 40/(20+40+80) = .2 * .28 = 5\%$$
$$G3 = 20/(20+80) * 80/(20+40+80) = .2 * .57 = 11\%$$

When *contractor001* switches AccountIDs, the next request will be processed by U1 or U2. At the present time, if all three Allocation Groups under R4 are active, the relative Performance Group weight for $H1$URGENT can vary across the two Allocation groups.

$$U1 = 80/(20+80) * 30/(30+60+90) = .8 * .16 = 12\%$$
$$U2 = 80/(20+80) * 60/(30+60+90) = .8 * .33 = 26\%$$

PERFORMANCE PERIODS

As shown earlier, each Performance Period defines a Milestone and an Allocation Group. A Milestone is made up of a Milestone Type and a Milestone Limit. The following chart explains their content.

Component	Definition
Milestone Type	The type of threshold used to define each Performance Period for a Performance Group. You can express types in the following units: • Time-of-day (T) • Session resource usage (S or R) • Query resource usage (Q)
Milestone Limit	The value of the threshold used to change Performance Periods for a Performance Group. You can express this value in the following units: • A valid time-of-day, such as 0800 for 8:00 a.m. • A number of seconds of CPU usage.
Allocation Group	The number of the Allocation Group used to control sessions during this Performance Period.

Figure 10.3

All Performance Periods within a Performance Group must use the Milestone Type.

When the threshold for the Performance Period is exceeded, the session is transferred to the next Performance Period, and the processes belonging to that session are placed under the control of a different Allocation Group. Typically, the change is to a lower-priority Allocation Group. Consequently access to resources will be progressively reduced for longer-running sessions. This is expressed in seconds to hundredths of a second, representing an amount of session CPU resource consumption per node.

Note: The compare and adjust concept monitors resource consumption and will modify queries that exceed threshold and that have been established by the workload parameters.

Time-of-day Performance Periods monitor the clock time, and optionally the day of the week. This is expressed in military time, representing time periods during a 24-hour day. For example, 0800 is 8:00 A.M. These types of Performance Periods are used to dynamically switch the Allocation Group of a session based on changes in business priority of different work at different times of day. For example, a session can be switched to a higher-priority Allocation Group after business hours or on weekends, when competition for database resources is not high.

CPU USAGE LIMITS WITH PRIORITY SCHEDULER

Priority Scheduler uses Milestones and CPU limits to manage CPU usage.

Milestones (either Query or Session) monitors CPU consumption for each query step and moves the query to another AG once the threshold is met. Milestones are time-based, you can limit a Resource Partition to a specified percentage of CPU resource usage.

CPU limits restrict CPU consumption on the system. This limit has no effect on the scheduling strategy defined by other Priority Scheduler parameters. The relative weights of Allocation Groups and Resource Partitions are observed. The normal distribution of resources prevails within the specified amount of CPU usage.

PERFORMANCE MONITORING TOOLS & FACILITIES

Note: You can also limit the percentage of total CPU usage by sessions controlled by an Allocation Group. The Milestone Limit of CPU usage is defined in seconds or fractions of seconds. Lastly, Milestones for SLES10 are only available on the appliance platform.

Schmon Utility

The schmon utility provides a command line interface that allows you to display and alter Priority Scheduler parameters.

Schmon runs on the following platforms and interfaces:

Platform	Interface
Windows	Command line ("Teradata Command Prompt") Database Window
Linux	Command line Database Window

Figure 10.4

If Workload Definitions have been activated using Teradata Viewpoint Workload Designer portlet, schmon cannot be used to modify the Priority Scheduler parameters.

Teradata Analyst Pack

There is a suite of software tools called the Teradata Analyst Pack. This suite of tools targets query or workload-based analysis and focuses on the execution performance at the individual query level. Tools include:

- Teradata Index Wizard

293

- Teradata Statistics Wizard
- Teradata Visual Explain
- Teradata System Emulation Tool

Visual Explain

Teradata Visual Explain is a tool (application) for analyzing query plans in a visual format. The discrete steps of the plan showing the flow of the data during execution are displayed in a graphical format.

To further aid DBAs as well as developers in their pursuit to optimize their queries, Visual Explain allows you to capture multiple plans in the same visual format and then compare them.

The first step for using Visual Explain is to create a Query Capture Database (QCD).

Once that is accomplished, the next step is to begin inserting query plans into the QCD.

A powerful feature of VE allows you to compare different versions of SQL statements. Once you have two or more query plans loaded into the QCD, you can use Visual Explain to select which plans to compare. Selecting the **Plans->Compare Report** . . . menu will cause VE to produce a series of reports for the chosen plans. The reports are as follows:

- Complete Information Report
- Teradata Database Configuration Report
- Step Information Report
- Estimated Cost Report
- Operation Report
- Operands Report
- Residual Condition Report

PERFORMANCE MONITORING TOOLS & FACILITIES

- Join Condition Report
- Join Order Report
- Source Attributes Report
- Target Attributes Report
- Indexes Used Report
- Index Condition Report

Note: One or more execution plans, visual plans, EXPLAIN text, or statement text can be saved to a file (*.vec*) (i.e. *offline* plan).

Statistics Wizard

Statistics Wizard can be utilized in automating the process of collecting statistics for a particular workload, indexes, and/or columns identified for collection/re-collection. You can also validate recommended statistics on the production system before applying in order to verify the performance of the proposed statistics.

Statistics Wizard provides the database administrator (DBA) with the following:

- Analyze a specified workload for recommendations to improve query performance in a workload.
- Select tables, indexes, or columns for arbitrary analysis, collection, or re-collection of statistics.
- Provide recommendations on specific workloads, table demographics, and basic heuristics.
- Schedule collection and dropping of statistics.
- Modify the interval for statistics collection on column or index.

As the database changes, Statistics Wizard can continue to provide analysis and recommendations on tables where statistics are needed. These are based on a number of data demographics such as age of data, table growth; along with identify columns/indexes that would improve with statistics for a specific workload. Finally, the DBA can either accept or reject the recommendations.

The steps for Best Practices are:

- Identify the set of SQL statements that must be analyzed for performance improvements.
- Define the identified set of SQL statements. This will be known as a workload.
- Run the statistics analysis.
- Validate the statistics.
- Apply or schedule the execution of the recommendations.

Like the Index Wizard, the first step is to define a workload. This can be done in the following ways.

- From DBQL Statements
- Using Statement Text
- From QCD Statements
- Importing a Workload
- From an Existing Workload

The reports available are:

This Report	Shows
Statistics Recommendations Report	Provides recommended statistics in the workload for tables.
Update Cost Analysis Report	The total number of statements within the workload based on a percentage that are UPDATE statements.
Table Usage Report	Show the frequency of access for a table within the workload.
Table Scan Report	Displays workload statistics on

PERFORMANCE MONITORING TOOLS & FACILITIES

This Report	Shows
	how a table is used based cardinality, AMP usage, and geography information.
Workload Analysis Report	Offers comparative cost estimates of a relative workload to the entire workload, statement text, frequency, and column types.

Figure 10.5

Index Wizard

Teradata Index Wizard is a front-end GUI client application that works the Parsing Engine optimizer component that enables this tool to compute, simulate, and evaluate candidates for index selection. This tool, which is installed with Microsoft Windows, empowers users with easy-to-use steps to define workload definitions, index analysis along with providing and reports for both operations. This is shown in the following illustration:

Teradata 14 Solutions Development

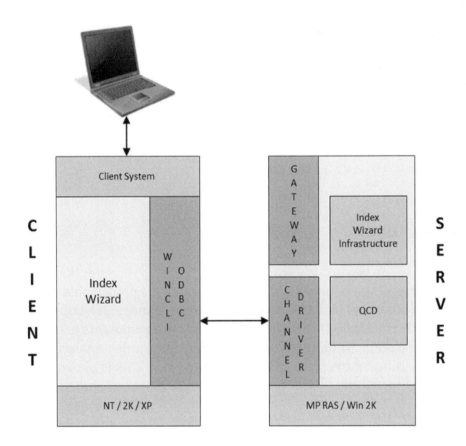

Figure 10.6

In addition, Teradata Index Wizard is integrated with the Database Query Log (DBQL). With this feature, you have the ability to analyze SQL statements that are collected in the query log, and based on the analysis; you can start to define workloads.

DBQL works with other client tools such as Teradata Statistics Wizard, Teradata System Emulation Tool, and Teradata Visual Explain. However, before you can create and analyze a workload using these tools, you must configure a Query Capture Database (QCD). Please see

PERFORMANCE MONITORING TOOLS & FACILITIES

the Teradata Visual Explain section in this chapter for setup and configuration steps.

Once defined, workloads can be imported for analysis on a test or development system before they are promoted to production. It can also be utilized to evaluate and simulate index recommendations on the production system before implementing.

Basic Index Wizard Steps

The following steps describe what you do:

1. Define a workload.

   A workload is a set of created or defined SQL statements using the workload definition dialog box. Index Wizard creates several workload reports utilizing the following components:

   - Using Database Query Log (DBQL)
   - Using statement text
   - From QCD statements
   - Importing workload
   - From an existing workload
   - Using Database XML Query Log (DBQL)

2. Workload is analyzed.

   Index Wizard may also recommend that indexes be added or dropped to enhance system performance after the workload is defined and analyzed.

   There are four types of analysis:

   - Index analysis
   - Partition analysis

- Restarting an analysis
- What-if analysis

3. Validates Index recommendations (optional).

   This feature is optional, but highly recommended because Index Wizard validates index recommendations on a production system without actually updating the production table index. This ensures the index recommendation will help database performance before actually adding the indexes.

4. Apply Index recommendations to the production system.

   You can execute an index immediately or schedule the execution at a different time / day after an index recommendation is validated.

The reports that are available are Workload Reports and Analysis Reports.

This Workload Report	Shows
Existing Indexes Report	This view displays information about the tables such as index types, unique flags, and index names.
Update Frequency Report	Provides percentage information on UPDATE statements on tables.
Table Usage Analysis Report	Information based on frequency in which the table is accessed within the workload.
Table Scan Report	This view displays usage information of a table. Parameters include cardinality, AMP usage, and geography information in the workload.
Workload Analysis Report	Provides estimates based on the

PERFORMANCE MONITORING TOOLS & FACILITIES

This Workload Report	Shows
	cost of a workload as it compares to the entire workload including statement text, frequency, and column types.
Object Global Use Count Report	Count information that identifies the objects that are most frequently accessed.

Figure 10.7

This Analysis Report...	Shows...
Index Recommendation Report	the recommended secondary index for each table if one is recommended.
Query Cost Analysis Report	the query cost of specific types of statements (SELECT, INSERT, DELETE) without the original recommended index and with the proposed recommended index.
Disk Space Analysis Report	the space estimate to store the recommended indexes
Summary Report	details about the secondary index counts and recommendation counts made in a specific analysis for all tables in the workload.
Index Maintenance Cost Report	the estimated cost of maintaining recommended indexes for a particular recommendation ID on a workload.

Figure 10.8

Index validation verifies if the recommended indexes will actually improve system performance. However, it does not execute the recommended indexes, but instead, uses the Parsing Engine Optimizer component to generate new plans with the recommended indexes.

Note: Index Wizard sample statistics saves them in the QCD. The sampled statistics are used for the index validation process.

The validation is conducted during the simulated session mode. This is where the recommendations for the indexes are tested for the plan generation. These recommendations are compared, analyzed, and validated on the set of SQL statements. The statements are submitted in a "no execute" phase, and the plans are saved into the QCD.

Validation can be done several ways:

Analysis performed on	Validation performed on
Production System	Production System
Test System	Production System
Production System	Test System (not recommended)
Test System	Test System (not recommended)

Figure 10.9

Index Wizard also has a feature that enables you to execute index recommendations immediately or schedule them for a later time, once the validation is completed.

Teradata System Emulation Tool (TSET)

Teradata SET (TSET) enables you to emulate a production system using a test system. Basically, system-level data is captured from the production system, and then imported into the test system. The Teradata Optimizer gathers information from the tables, along with appropriate column and index statistics, in order to build query plans on a test system that can simulate as the production environment.

The following diagram illustrates the relationship between TSET, target systems, and test systems.

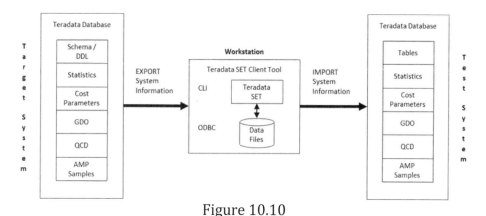

Figure 10.10

Imported data is used to:

- Simulate Optimizer performance of the production system. Execution plans are generated based on several factors including indexes, primary and secondary keys, and available statistics and resources. These factors provide the Optimizer with an accurate execution plan.
- Create query plans that emulate the target system under a variety of conditions. A small test system can be used to create query plans that simulate a production system.
- Conduct *what-if scenarios*.
- Resolve and test Optimizer-related performance scenarios that might occur on the production system.

Note: Teradata Visual Explain can use TSET to simulate how a production system will perform under specific conditions and workloads.

TSET also synchronizes all of the configuration settings, databases, data models, and data dependencies to maintain the correct relationships when exported and imported. In addition, database objects such as tables, views, macros, triggers, join indexes, and stored procedures are duplicated on the test system and function as if they were on the production system. The use of TSET enables users to thoroughly debug and optimize queries in a safe, but equivalent simulated environment before integrating them into production.

Prior to performing export operations, make sure the access rights are set. The SHOW QUALIFIED SQL statement and configuration data (Random AMP Sample (RAS), statistics, object definitions) is required in order for these objects to be returned from this statement and exported.

The following table lists the access rights required to export each type of information.

Exported Information	Required Rights
Cost parameters	INSERT, SELECT, and DELETE on *SystemFE.Opt_Cost_Table* and *SystemFE.Opt_DBSCtl_Table*.
Execution plans	For an existing plan: • SELECT on the QCD tables or on the QCD • EXECUTE on QCD macros DUMP EXPLAIN right for a new query. For a new plans with accompanied demographics: • INSERT EXPLAIN statement for the given query • EXECUTE on the QCD macros.
Object definitions	SHOW statement for join indexes, macros, tables, triggers, stored procedures, and User-Defined Types (UDTs).

PERFORMANCE MONITORING TOOLS & FACILITIES

Exported Information	Required Rights
	SELECT and SHOW QUALIFIED to export object definitions for a view statement. SELECT on DBC.ColumnsV and DBC.TablesV to export databases and referenced UDTs.
Machine configuration	MONRESOURCE on the database.
RAS	SELECT for tables for export. INSERT, SELECT, and DELETE on *SystemFE.Opt_RAS_Table*.
Statistics	HELP STATISTICS on the tables or join index referenced. SELECT on the DBC.IndexStatsV, DBC.ColumnStatsV, and DBC.MultiColumnStatsV views.
Demographics	SELECT on the data demographics table and related views of the table. COLLECT DEMOGRAPHICS statement on the tables indentified, SELECT on QCD views. EXECUTE on QCD macros.
QCD data	SELECT on QCD tables and views. EXECUTE on QCD macros.
Workloads	SELECT on QCD tables and views. EXECUTE on QCD macros.
Cost profiles	SELECT on the DBC.CostProfiles_v and DBC.CostProfileValues_v views.

Figure 10.11

Set access rights prior to performing import operations. The following table lists the access rights required to import each type of information.

Imported Information	Required Rights
Cost parameters	INSERT access on *SystemFE.Opt_Cost_Table* and *SystemFE.Opt_DBSCtl_Table*.
Execution plans	INSERT, SELECT, and UPDATE on tables and views for the QCD database.
Object definitions	CREATE access on the user or database for objects being imported. CREATE PROCEDURE WITH GRANT OPTION for the stored procedures on the database. UDTTYPE access on the SYSUDTLIB database for creating the UDT. UDTUSAGE access to CREATE TABLE statement for the UDT.
RAS	INSERT on *SystemFE.Opt_RAS_Table*.
Statistics	COLLECT STATISTICS privileges for all tables or join indexes referenced.
Demographics	INSERT, SELECT, and UPDATE on the table and associated views. EXECUTE for macros.
QCD data	INSERT, SELECT, and UPDATE on QCD tables. SELECT on QCD views.
Workloads	INSERT, SELECT, and UPDATE on QCD tables.

PERFORMANCE MONITORING TOOLS & FACILITIES

Imported Information	Required Rights
	SELECT on QCD views.
Cost profiles	EXECUTE on the DBC.CreateNewCostProfile and DBC.InsertConstantValue macros.

Figure 10.12

The next table lists the access rights required in order to restore the default test system environment (also known as *undo-import* or *cleanup* operations).

Undo-Import Information	Required Rights
Cost parameters	DELETE on *SystemFE.Opt_Cost_Table* and *SystemFE.Opt_DBSCtl_Table* or on the SystemFE object.
Execution plans	DELETE on the tables or on the QCD database. EXECUTE on QCD macros.
Object definitions	DROP or DELETE rights on the parent database or object.
RAS	DELETE on *SystemFE.Opt_RAS_Table* or on the SystemFE database.
Statistics	DROP STATISTICS privileges for the tables or join indexes referenced.
Demographics	DELETE on the tables and the associated views of the table. EXECUTE on macros.
QCD data	DELETE on tables and views. EXECUTE on macros.
Workloads	DELETE on tables and views. EXECUTE on macros.

Undo-Import Information	Required Rights
Cost profiles	EXECUTE on the DBC.DeleteCostProfile macro.

Figure 10.13

The Export feature of TSET can be customized to ensure that the test system imitates the features of the target system being analyzed. The following topics explain how to capture information from a target system.

Export by Query

This export option identifies database objects to export via DML statements. The export-by-query, through the use of DML statements as input, uses the SHOW QUALIFIED statement.

Note: Data Definition Language (DDL) statements are not used with the export-by-query option.

The SHOW QUALIFIED command returns the CREATE VIEW text and the CREATE TABLE text of any tables referenced by the view.

Export by Database

Use the export-by-database method to select database objects for individual export and to define the information to export.

Export by Workload

Export by workload is used to export multiple workloads and the specified QCD database along with capture the definition details for emulation.

Perform Query Testing

TSET is used to execute and test SQL statements before they are productionized. This can be done through Execute SQL main window or Teradata SQL Assistant.

ResUsage

Resource usage data is stored on several tables located in the DBC database. There are views and macros available for reporting on the resource usage data that is stored.

You can also write your own queries or macros on resource usage data. As with other database data, you can access resource usage data using SQL.

You need to decide what resource usage data you want to collect and the level of detail you want it to cover. Once you set up your resource usage data collection the way you want, the only maintenance required is to purge old data regularly. The following table is an overview of the information covered by resource usage data:

Resource usage data covers	Which includes
BYNET traffic on a node	Messaging includes point-to-point, broadcast, and merge activities.
client-to-server traffic	Data on each communication link.
CPU utilization	Overhead, user service, and time of session execution.
data tracking	Status of sessions in locking queues.
logical device traffic (SCSI)	Count of reads/writes and amount of data transferred as seen from the SCSI driver.
vdisk logical device traffic	All the cylinders allocated by an AMP.

Teradata 14 Solutions Development

Resource usage data covers	Which includes
Priority Scheduler information	Resuage data captured by Performance Group (PG) from Priority Scheduler and reported by Teradata Active System Management (Teradata ASM) workloads (WDs).
AMP Worker Task (AWT) Information	AWT statistics.
memory management activity	Memory allocation, aging, paging, and swapping.
summary information	All data collected for a node or vproc.

Figure 10.14

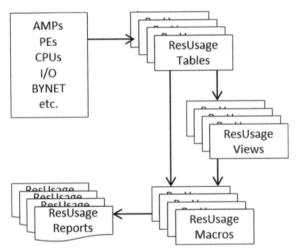

Figure 10.15

PERFORMANCE MONITORING TOOLS & FACILITIES

ResUsage Tables

Node Resource Usage Tables	
ResUsageSpma *System-wide node information*	**ResUsageScpu** *Information specific to the CPUs within the nodes*
Vproc Resource Usage Tables	
ResUsageSawt *AWT statistics*	**ResUsageShst** *Channel and LAN communication info*
ResUsageSldv *System-wide logical device info*	**ResUsageSpdsk** *Includes Virtual Storage resource usage logs on cylinder I/O, allocation, and migration*
ResUsageSps *Priority Scheduler Performance Group data*	**ResUsageSvdsk** *AMP-level vdisk statistics*
ResUsageSvpr *System-wide vproc information*	

Figure 10.16

Node Resource Usage Tables		
The tables in this group are controlled by the RSS Collection Rate and Node logging rate.		
Table Name	**Covers**	**When You Should Enable**
ResUsageScpu	Statistics on the CPUs within the nodes.	When analysis indicates that the overall performance is limited on an individual processor. For example, a specific CPU on each node or a specific node is active while other CPUs are idle which could indicate a

Table Name	Covers	When You Should Enable
		process uses that CPU consistently. Note: When first implemented, you should enable this table to verify the following: • Verify all CPUs are functioning correctly • Check the load balance among the CPUs
ResUsageSpma	Provided node summary information of overall system-wide utilization. This also integrates information from of the other tables.	This captures the operational history of the system. This table also captures information on BYNET utilization.
ResUsageIpma	System-wide Internal node information	Generally, this table is not used at customer sites. Used by Teradata Engineering.

Figure 10.17

Vproc Resource Usage Tables		
The tables in this group are controlled by the RSS Collection Rate and the Vproc logging rate.		
Table Name	Covers	When You Should Enable
ResUsageSawt	Data specific to the AMP worker tasks (AWTs).	Provides the ability to monitor AWTs utilization and whether there is a backlog of work because

PERFORMANCE MONITORING TOOLS & FACILITIES

Table Name	Covers	When You Should Enable
		the AWTs are all being utilized.
ResUsageShst	Channel statistics on the host and LANs that communicate with Teradata Database.	To capture information about the traffic over the IBM Host and LAN channels to determine if there is a bottleneck.
ResUsageSldv	System-wide, logical device statistics collected from the SCSI bus.	To analyze utilization statistics for disk usage.
ResUsageSps	Data by Performance Group (PG) ID from the Priority Scheduler.	Used to track utilization by the query Workload Definition (WD) level.
ResUsageSvdsk	Statistics collected from the vdisk logical device.	To view the details of the disk usage across the AMPs to look for hot AMPS or other skew issues.
ResUsageSvpr	Data specific to each vpoc and file system.	Provides resource details being utilized by each vproc on the system. Good for investigating hot AMPS or PEs that may be CPU bound.
ResUsageIvpr	System-wide internal vproc processor information,	Generally, this table is not used at customer sites. Used by Teradata Engineering.

Figure 10.18

ResUsage Views
DBC.ResGeneralInfoView

TheDate	TheTime	Secs
NodeId	GroupId	NCPUs
CPUBusy	CPUOpSys	CPUUser
CPUWaitIO	DiskSegmentIO	LogicalDeviceIO
LogicalDeviceReads	LogicalDeviceWrites	LogicalDeviceReadKB
LogicalDeviceWriteKB	MemAgings	MemCtxtPageReads
MemCtxtPageWrites	MemFails	MemFreeKB
MemProcSwapped	MemSize	MemSwapDropKB
MemSwapDrops	MemSwapReadKB	MemSwapReads
MemTextAllocs	MemTextPageDrops	MemTextPageReads
MemVprAllocs	MemVprAllocKB	NetAttempts
NetBackoffs	NetChannelSR	NetMultiIO
NetPtoPIO	NetReadKB	NetReads
NetWriteKB	NetWrites	NetRxConnected
NetTxConnected	NetTxRouting	NetTxIdle
NetRxIdle	NetSamples	PageOrSwapIO
ProcActiveAvg	ProcBlksDBLock	ProcBlockedAvg
ProcBlocks	ProcWaits	UserStmtsArriving
UserStmtsInProgress		

Figure 10.19

PERFORMANCE MONITORING TOOLS & FACILITIES

DBC.ResCPUUsageByAMPView

TheDate	TheTime	Vproc
NodeId	Secs	NCPUs
GroupId	AMPWorkTaskExec	AMPWorkTaskServ
AMPMiscUserExec	AMPMiscUserServ	AMPTotalUserExec
AMPTotalUserServ		

Figure 10.20

DBC.ResCPUUsageByPEView

TheDate	TheTime	Vproc
NodeId	Secs	NCPUs
GroupId	PEDispExec	PEDispServ
PEParsExec	PEParsServ	PESessExec
PESessServ	PEMiscUserExec	PEMiscUserServ
PETotalUserExec	PETotalUserServ	

Figure 10.21

DBC.ResShstGroupView

TheDate	TheTime	NodeId
VprId	HstId	HstType
Secs	NominalSecs	GroupId
CollectIntervals	HostBlockReads	HostBlockWrites
HostMessageReads	HostMessageWrites	HostReadKB
HostWriteKB	HostQLenSum	HostQLenMax
HostReadFails	HostWriteFails	

Figure 10.22

DBC.ResSldvGroupView

TheDate	TheTime	NodeId
VprId	LdvId	LdvType
Secs	NominalSecs	GroupId
CollectIntervals	LdvOutReqSum	LdvReads
LdvWrites	LdvReadKB	LdvWriteKB
LdvReadRespTot	LdvWriteRespTot	LdvReadRespMax
LdvWriteRespMax	LdvConcurrentMax	LdvOutReqMax
LdvOutReqTime		

Figure 10.23

ResUsage Macros

These macros	Provide the following.
ResAWT	Reports the average AMP Worker Task in use for all AMPs in the system.
ResAWTByAMP	Reports the average AMP Worker Task in use for each AMP.
ResAWTByNode	Reports the average AMP Worker Task on all AMPs in each node.

Figure 10.24

These macros	Provide the following.
ResCPUByAMP	Reports how each AMP on each node utilizes the CPUs.
ResCPUByAMPOneNode	Reports how each AMP on a specific node utilizes the CPUs.
ResAmpCpuByGroup	Reports the summary of AMP CPU usage by node grouping.

Figure 10.25

PERFORMANCE MONITORING TOOLS & FACILITIES

These macros	Provide the following.
ResCPUByPE	Reports how each PE on each node is utilizing the CPUs.
ResCPUByPEOneNode	Reports how each PE on a specific node is utilizing the CPUs.
ResPeCpuByGroup	Reports the PE CPU utilization summarized by a node grouping.

Figure 10.26

These macros	Provide the following.
ResCPUByNode	Reports how each individual node is utilizing its CPUs.
ResCPUOneNode	Reports how a specific node is utilizing its CPUs.
ResCPUByGroup	Reports how a specified Node Group is utilizing the system CPUs.

Figure 10.27

These macros	Provide the following.
ResHostByLink	Reports the host traffic for every communication link in the system.
ResHostOneNode	Reports the host traffic for the communication links of a specific node.
ResHostByGroup	Reports the host traffic for the communication links of a node grouping.

Figure 10.28

These macros	Provide the following.
ResLdvByNode	Reports the logical device traffic channeled through each node by totaling its controller links into one summarized node output line.
ResLdvOneNode	Reports the logical device traffic channeled through a specific node by totaling all of its controller links into one summarized node output line.
ResLdvByGroup	Reports the logical device traffic channeled through a node grouping.

Figure 10.29

These macros	Provide the following.
ResMemMgmtByNode	Reports memory management activity for each individual node.
ResMemMgmtOneNode	Reports memory management activity for a specific node.
ResMemByGroup	Reports memory management activity for a node grouping.

Figure 10.30

These macros	Provide the following.
ResNetByNode	Reports net traffic for each node.
ResNetOneNode	Reports net traffic for a specific node.
ResNetByGroup	Reports net traffic for nodes summarized by node groups.

Figure 10.31

PERFORMANCE MONITORING TOOLS & FACILITIES

These macros	Provide the following.
ResNode	Provides a summary of resource usage averaged across all nodes, excluding any PE-only nodes.
ResOneNode	Provides a summary of resource usage by returning the node requested.
ResNodeByNode	Provides a summary of resource usage by returning the nodes requested.
ResNodeByGroup	Provides a summary of resource usage by defined groups of nodes.

Figure 10.32

These macros	Provide the following.
ResPdskByNode	Reports the device traffic by a physical node.
ResPdskOneNode	Reports the device traffic for a specified node.
ResPsByNodeWDJoin	aggregated by all AMPs in an individual node and Allocation Group ID, produces one row of data for each workload and performance period combination, for each logging period.
ResPsWDJoin	aggregated by all AMPs for all nodes in the system.

Figure 10.33

These macros	Provide the following.
ResPsCPU	a summary of Teradata ASM workload CPU use versus the relative weights of their associated Allocation Groups.
ResPsCPUByNodeWDJoin	the summary of CPU usage by node, Allocation Group, and workload as compared to the real-time relative weight of each Allocation Group.
ResPsCPUWDJoin	the summary of CPU usage for all nodes, Allocation Groups, and workloads in the system as compared to the real-time relative weight of each Allocation Group.

Figure 10.34

These macros	Provide the following.
ResVdskByNode	Reports the logical device traffic by a physical node.
ResVdskOneNode	Reports the logical device traffic for a specified node.
ResVdskByGroup	Reports the logical device traffic by a node grouping.

Figure 10.35

Specifying ResUsage Tables and Logging Rates

The default collection and logging settings provide a good start for basic system monitoring. The default results in the ResUsageSpma (SPMA) table being logged every 10 minutes (600 seconds).

The applications that use the collect buffer generally require more frequent data updates; therefore, the collection rate is typically

PERFORMANCE MONITORING TOOLS & FACILITIES

adjusted to 60 seconds. Viewpoint and PM/API, do not require the logging rate to be changed or any of the tables to be enabled for logging in order to access the RSS data they use.

The ResUsageSpma table provides a high level summary of how the system is operating and contains summarized or key elements from most of the other tables. If you want to record detailed statistics covered by any of the ResUsage tables, then you should enable them for logging, along with specifying the largest logging period that will meet your needs. You should not log data that you do not have a planned need for since this does incur additional database system overhead and uses up additional database space.

Naturally, the more tables you enable for logging and the shorter the logging period used, the more overhead the system will use.

You can use the Teradata Viewpoint Remote Console, or ctl to enable or disable the ResUsage tables.

Populating the ResUsage Tables

Resource usage data gathering is a two-phase process as follows:

- Data collection

  During the data collection phase the RSS gathers information from the operating system, Parallel Database Extensions (PDE), and Teradata Database.

  Data collection continues for a user-specified period of time, called the collection interval.

- Data logging

In the logging phase, which occurs at the end of each logging period and consists of one or more complete collect intervals, the RSS writes all gathered data to ResUsage tables and reinitializes the shared data collection buffers for the next log interval.

PERFORMANCE MONITORING TOOLS & FACILITIES

The following diagram illustrates this:

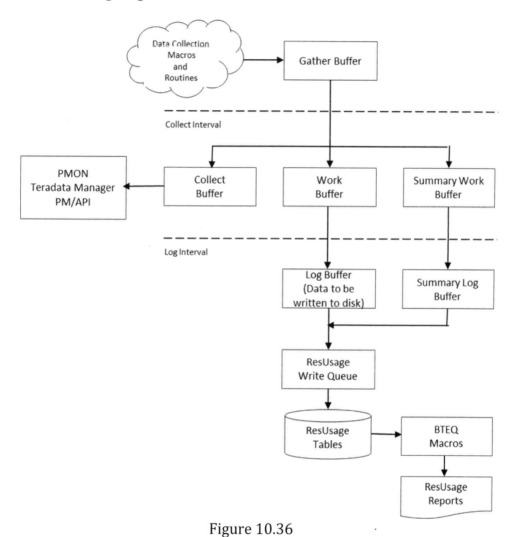

Figure 10.36

Locking Logger

The Locking Logger utility (dumplocklog) creates a table that stores lock information that is extracted from transaction logs on the Teradata Database. This information can be utilized to analyze lock contentions and whether system performance has been degraded by an inappropriate mix of SQL statements.

When logging is enabled, each AMP will create a memory buffer for saving transaction locking information. The locking logger will also capture information for global deadlocks such as Host Utility (HUT) locks.

The lock log buffer default size is 64 KB. When full, the previous log is overwritten. This provides an updated log of the transaction locks encountered on each AMP. This value indicates the size of the locking logger segments. The lock log segment size is divided into two parts: main and partial. The last 32 KB of the lock log segment is the partial part and contains global deadlock information. Both parts contain information about the locks.

Note: This buffer can be changed by modifying the LockLogSegmentSize field in the DBS Control record from 64 to 1024 KB.

When a lock contention delay is encountered by a transaction, the AMP writes an entry into the buffer. The following information concerning the delayed transaction is recorded:

- The date and time of the requested transaction lock
- The length of time the blocked transaction was blocked
- The database and table information which the lock was requested
- The host ID and session number of the requested transaction lock

PERFORMANCE MONITORING TOOLS & FACILITIES

- The host ID and session number of the transaction that caused the lock
- The AMP vproc where the lock was requested
- The lock level (database, table, row, or range of rows), and type (read, write, exclusive), of the requested lock
- The type of DML statement transaction (INSERT, UPDATE, SELECT, and so forth)
- Indication if the lock caused a deadlock

The lock log table allows you to define the information that you want to retrieve from the lock log buffers. When using Locking Logger to create a lock log table, you must provide the following information:

- User name and password
- Number of SQL sessions Locking Logger will use to perform the INSERT operations. The minimum is one session. The maximum is one session for each online AMP, but is limited by the number of PEs.

If Locking Logger runs in continuous mode then there should be a minimum of one free console session available per PE. There is a limit of 6 console sessions per PE vproc. Depending on what's running, sometimes there are not enough of these sessions per AMP to invoke the Locking Logger utility. Basically, you cannot risk taking console sessions from other more important jobs (i.e. load utilities). However, you are unable to adjust the number of sessions dynamically once the value is set. Therefore, you need to configure this based upon activation. This number should leave enough sessions available for other utilities and provides sufficient parallelism for Locking Logger's to insert rows.

If Locking Logger runs in snapshot mode, then you will need one or more console PE sessions available in order for Locking Logger to run.

Use the Lock Log table along with the DBC.EventLog table to determine the blocked user from the blocking user.

DBC.AMPUsage

The DBC.AMPUsage view provides information about the usage of each AMP for each user and account. It also tracks the activities of any console utilities. By user, account, or console utility session, DBC.AMPUsage stores information about:

- CPU time consumed
- Number of read/write (I/O) operations generated

AMPUsage reports logical I/Os explicitly requested by the database software, even if the requested segment is in cache and no physical I/O is performed.

Use the information provided by DBC.AMPUsage to do the following:

- Bill an account for system resource use.
- Determine what resources were used, by user and/or account, by hour, shift, day, or week
- Summarize and archive after etc… on a per hour, per shift or per day basis.
- Determine if one or more queries had skewed processing (you would like to see if tables were skewed)
- Determine which session caused reduced performance.
- Derive capacity needs to plan for expansion.
- Account String Expansion (ASE) variables are also encouraged in the account string for the most useful logging in AMPUsage

Note: All of the items in the list require a well-defined account string to accomplish the above.

PERFORMANCE MONITORING TOOLS & FACILITIES

The DBC.AMPUsage view displays CPU usage information differently than the way such information is displayed in resource usage data.

The following chart summarizes the difference.

This facility	Provides
ResUsage	Metrics on the whole system, without making distinctions by individual user or account ID.
DBC.AMPUsageV view	AMP usage by individual user or account ID. Some CPU used for the system cannot be accounted for in AMPUsage. Therefore, ResUsage CPU metrics will always be larger than AMPUsage metrics. Typically, AMPUsage captures about 70- 90% of ResUsage CPU time.

Figure 10.37

Teradata 14 Solutions Development

Chapter 10: Practice Questions

1. An Access Logging entry indicates what?
   a. the statement was performed
   b. a privilege check was done

2. Which of the following collects the SQL information?
   a. Access logging
   b. Query logging

3. Which applications allow you to build your own workload definitions?
   a. Index Wizard
   b. Statistics Wizard
   c. Visual Explain
   d. Workload Analyzer

Use the following information to answer questions 6, 7, and 8.

GIVEN: Four Resource Partitions with individual weight assignments of R1 = 10, R2 = 20, R3 = 40, R4= 80, and four Allocation Groups under R3 with individual weight assignments of U1 = 10, U2 = 20, U3 = 40, U4 = 80.

4. If R3 and U1 are currently active, U1 will get ____ of the system's resources.
   a. 25%
   b. 35%
   c. 50%
   d. 100%

5. If R1 and R3 are currently active, and U1 and U3 are currently active, U3 is getting _____ of R3's resources.
    a. 10%
    b. 20%
    c. 40%
    d. 80%

6. If R2 and R3 are currently active, and U3 and U4 are currently active, U4 is getting _____ of the system's resources.
    a. 12%
    b. 21%
    c. 37%
    d. 54%

7. You _____ convert Priority Definition sets to Workload Definition sets.
    a. can
    b. cannot

8. The maximum number of Performance Periods within a Performance Group is ____.
    a. 2
    b. 4
    c. 6
    d. 8

9. Visual Explain requires the creation of a _____ database.
    a. DB2
    b. QED
    c. QDC
    d. QCD
    e. DBA

Teradata 14 Solutions Development

10. Where should the validation of index analysis provided by Index Wizard be done?
    a. Production system
    b. Test system

11. Viewpoint and PM/API get ResUsage data from which buffer?
    a. Collect buffer
    b. Gather buffer
    c. Work buffer
    d. Summary work buffer

12. When lock logging is enabled, who keeps track of all locks in the system?
    a. The PE of the user.
    b. A single AMP.
    c. Each individual AMP.

13. Locking Logger can run in _____ mode.
    a. one shot or snapshot
    b. snapshot or continuous
    c. peek or capture

14. AMPUsage reports which of the following?
    a. Logical I/O
    b. Physical I/O
    c. Both Physical I/O and Logical I/O

PERFORMANCE MONITORING TOOLS & FACILITIES

Chapter Notes

Utilize this space for notes, key points to remember, diagrams, areas of further study, etc.

Chapter 11 - Solution Planning

Certification Objectives

- ✓ Given a scenario, verify that a proposed solution addresses the requirements.
- ✓ Identify the tools and features available to implement and manage application security and privacy.
- ✓ When planning for implementation of a new solution, identify the information that should be provided to the capacity planning process.
- ✓ When planning for implementation of a new solution, identify the information that should be provided to the security planning process.
- ✓ When planning for implementation of a new solution, identify the information that should be provided to the data warehouse administration planning process.
- ✓ Describe a process to promote from development, to test environment(s), and into production.
- ✓ Identify components for a dual system architecture.

Before You Begin

You should be familiar with the following terms and concepts.

Terms	Key Concepts
Implementation Planning	Capacity, Security, Administration
Optimization Analysis	WHERE clause, EXPLAIN, heartbeat queries, performance (current vs. historical). table design, failure recovery, dual systems

Capacity planning

When beginning to plan for capacity of a new Teradata implementation, you should always plan towards making the data that is most frequently accessed available at all times and retrieval as efficient as possible. The idea of data having a temperature is used to help define what data is most frequently accessed (Hot) to data that is only very rarely accessed (Cold). Data in between those extremes is considered Warm. Additionally, due to regulatory concerns, such as Sarbanes-Oxley, there are instances where very large amounts of data are retained for very long periods and almost never accessed. This data is considered to be dormant, or Icy.

Once you have determined the different temperatures of your data, you will need to analyze how it will be stored physically. There are far too many nuances to designing an efficient Teradata database to be covered here. However, here are some general considerations to be mindful of:

- Each row in a table has overhead above and beyond the space needed to store the actual data.
- Column partitioned tables store their data by placing the data within a series of containers or subrows, depending on the storage format.
- Each table in a Teradata database has an associated subtable stored on each AMP in the system. These subtables are called Table Headers.
- Space in the database can be saved by utilizing a few common techniques while defining columns of tables:
  - Using Multi-Value Compression where commonly occurring values in a field are compressed to save space.
  - Using VARCHAR instead of a compressed CHARACTER data type.
  - Be thoughtful about the precision used when defining columns as DECIMAL and INTEGER.

SOLUTION PLANNING

- Secondary, Join, and Hash Indexes all require subtables to store their data.
- Spool Space is critical to the operations of the data warehouse. It is taken from disks that are not currently being used for data. This means that if you do not have enough disk space in your Teradata database, you risk not having enough Spool Space and therefore unable to run large queries.
- TEMP space is also critical for users to perform certain tasks and should be accounted for as well.
- Allowing for Backup space is also of vital importance obviously.

Each data disk in a Teradata system is broken down into segments in a way similar to below:

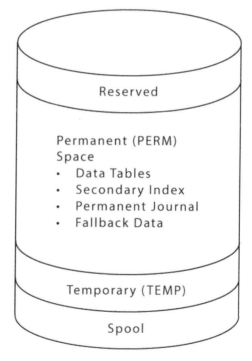

Figure 11.1

Security planning

Defining a Security Policy

Your security policy should be based on the following considerations:

- Determine your security needs to balance the need for secure data against user needs for quick and efficient data access.
- Review Teradata Database security features to meet your needs.
- Develop a security strategy that includes both system-enforced and personnel-enforced security features.

Publishing a Security Policy

To ensure administrators and users at your site understand and follow site-specific security procedures, the administrator should create a security handbook.

The handbook should summarize how you are using Teradata Database security features for your database. You should include the following topics in this document:

- Why security is needed.
- Benefits of adhering to the security policy for both the company and the users.
- A description of the specific implementation of Teradata Database security features at your site.
- Suggested/required security actions for users and administrators to follow.
- Who to contact when security questions arise.

SOLUTION PLANNING

The following summarize the security features provided by Teradata.

Security library

- A set of pre-configured security mechanisms.
- Editable configuration files that allow you to revise mechanism properties to meet unique security needs.
- A set of tools and interfaces for configuring and managing network security functions.

Security features

- Security Mechanism: A mechanism selected at logon to set the security context for the session. Each security mechanism defines a unique security context. Examples of this would include:
    - Kerberos (KRB5)
    - Kerberos (KRB5C)
    - LDAP
    - Roles

- User Authentication: Verification of user identity at logon. The system checks user name, password, and other optional user information against user data stored in the database. Only valid users can access the database. User Authentication methodologies would be as follows:

    - Logon formats and controls
        - Command line
        - Graphical User Interface (GUI)
    - Password format and controls
    - Optional user authentication by external applications

- User Authorization: Authorization of users specifically granted privileges to create, alter, or delete data in the database. The system evaluates user SQL requests to perform such functions and authorizes user activity according to access privileges defined for that user in the database. The mechanisms for User Authorization are as follows:

- o Implicit Privileges
- o Explicit Privileges
- o Inherited Privileges

- Encryption: Data transmitted across the network is encoded by the system to provide confidentiality. Typical process for Encryption would include:

  - o Logon Encryption
  - o Message Encryption

- Data Integrity: The system checks messages against what was sent to ensure that data has not been lost or corrupted during transmission across the network. An example would be as follows:

  - o Teradata Database performs an automatic check of data integrity for all message transmissions (both encrypted and non-encrypted) across the network to ensure that data has not been changed, corrupted, or lost during transmission.

- Directory Management of Users: Supported directories can be configured to authenticate users and authorized database access privileges. Below is an example of this feature:

  - o Normally, users that log on to Teradata Database have been defined in the database using a CREATE USER request. However, because many potential database users may already be defined in a directory running within the client network, Teradata Database allows for authentication and authorization of users by supported directories. Integration of directory managed users simplifies administration by eliminating the need to create a database instance for every user.

- Monitoring Access to the Database: Provides the ability to monitor database activity to identify violations, violators, and potential security hazards. The following outlines how you can Monitors Database Access:

    o Teradata Database automatically tracks all logon and logoff activity and stores this information in the DBC Data Dictionary Directory. That said, you can apply certain Teradata Database features to specify additional audits of specific events in Teradata Database. Monitoring can help identify the following security hazards:

        - Potential break-ins.
        - Attempts to gain unauthorized access to database resources.
        - Attempts to alter the behavior of Teradata Database auditing functions.

    o The security monitoring features can help you examine or print audit data during normal operation hours, or you can archive the data for later review by means of automated views and generated reports.

- Traditionally, access for users has been primarily at the object level, such as view or table. Teradata also offers Row Level Security to provide the ability to control access for users for each row in a table.

Migration Planning

Migrating to Teradata from another RDBMS can be challenging but, if done correctly, will provide for a much improved and extensible data warehouse. Teradata provides services for migrating from most of the major RDBMS vendors or a team can decide to take on the task themselves. In order to have a successful transition, there are many tasks that need to be completed. Below you will find some of the most critical of those tasks:

- Understand the architectural differences between the old RDBMS and Teradata. It is of the utmost importance that these differences be identified and understood by the entire team working on the migration.
- Have a full accounting of the existing data warehouse. You cannot begin to plan the new data warehouse until you know what is in your old RDBMS, how it is being used, and what its shortcomings are prompting the migration to Teradata.
- Requirements Analysis is the process of taking the information you have compiled about the old system and merging it with information you gather about how the new Teradata system will be used along with any new data sources.
- Once the requirements have been gathered, you can begin the Logical Data Modeling (LDM) process. This is where you start to identify the objects and their relationships.
- Teradata adds a step to the design process that they call Activity Transaction Modeling (ATM). During this step, you will begin to attach physical attributes to the LDM by identifying business rules, applications that will use the data warehouse, transactions, data demographics, attribute domains, etc..
- Once the LDM and ATM are completed, the Physical Data Model (PDM) can be derived. This is where you take the information gathered in previous steps and begin to make it a physical reality by identifying and creating actual databases, tables, views, macros, etc..

SOLUTION PLANNING

- After the actual database objects have been created, you can develop and initiate the processes for extracting the data from the old RDBMS to the new Teradata data warehouse. There are many ways to do this and are dependent on the specifics of the situation.

Administration planning

Keep and utilize performance data history to maintain efficient use of existing system resources. Typically applications would include:

- Maximizing system resources by scheduling for large query jobs, or backup/restore activities during available idle cycles.

- Managing resources to meet pent-up demand that may peak during prime hours ensures that the system operates efficiently to meet workload-specific goals.

Data integration

Teradata Warehouse is able to integrate itself into enterprise business and technical architectures, especially those that support business users, partners, and customers. This simplifies the task of coordinating enterprise applications and business processes.

For example, a Teradata event, generated from a database trigger, calls an external stored procedure. It publishes a message via a WebSphere MQ-Series message bus. The message is delivered to a JMS queue on a Web Logic application server. The Teradata Database receives the JMS message, notifies the user via their UI and activates a service or schedules a job for later execution.

Note: The success, or failure, depends upon how normalized, or denormalized, your data model is.

Design For Decision Support and Tactical Analysis, Not OLTP Applications

Not only is basic schema normalization an important design consideration, but normalization tailored specifically for the analytical needs of business intelligence is also critical. Even fully normalized data warehouses are often built as if they were designed to support OLTP applications.

Designers often fail to examine the following list of considerations:

- Integration of subject areas
- Versioning across time
- Generalization of key entities in anticipation of change
- Interrelation of life cycles across many cross-subject area entities and events
- Integration of measures, calculations, and dimensional context paths across the enterprise

These factors all support the immediate and long-term benefits provided by a fully normalized enterprise data model. The fully normalized schema provides a framework both for continued growth and for increasing user insight.

Design for Flexible Access Using Views

You should design your applications to always access the data warehouse through views rather than directly accessing base tables. View projections of the base tables can minimize the use of spool space by joins by reducing the number of columns that must be redistributed to make the join. Furthermore, you can more readily control locking for access through careful view design, and so minimize the complexity of applications that access the database through those views.

Data access

For Capacity Planning

If performance degradation is a gradual consequence of increased growth or higher performance expectations, all data collected over time can be used for capacity or other proactive planning. Since the onset of growth-related performance degradation can often be insidious, taking measurements and tracking both data and usage growth can be very useful.

Managing performance yields efficient use of existing system resources and can guide capacity planning activities along sound and definable lines.

Performance metrics

To Help Identify System Problems

Managing performance helps system administrators identify system problems.

Managing performance includes, among other things, monitoring system performance through real-time alerts and by tracking performance historically. Being able to react to changes in system performance quickly and knowledgeably ensures the efficient availability of the system. Troubleshooting rests on sound system monitoring.

STEPS REQUIRED FOR ANALYZING QUERIES FOR OPTIMIZATION

WHERE clause analysis

Obviously, all JOIN columns should have statistics collected on them. Columns, whether indexed or not, appearing in a WHERE clause should have statistics collected on them as well.

The Optimizer is not affected by the order of tests in a WHERE clause. As an example, A = 10 AND B = 300, AND C = 'XYZ' is the same as B = 300 AND A = 10 AND C = 'XYZ, which is the same as C = 'XYZ' AND A = 10 AND B = 300, which is the same as . . .

The important thing is whether statistics on the columns are available. Without statistics, the Parser is very conservative. With statistics, it is far more aggressive.

Though the WHERE clause limits the number of rows appearing in Spool, the number of columns being projected, and their data type size, determine the width of Spool rows.

Explains

Use of the EXPLAIN modifier, or Visual Explain, will show the retrieval paths chosen by the Parser. Modifying the structure of the tables will change performance. As an example:

- Changing a UPI/NUSI to a NUPI/USI
- Creating/dropping SIs
- Collecting/refreshing statistics
- Creating/dropping Join Indexes
- Creating/dropping Partitioned Primary Indexes
- Creating/dropping Hash Indexes
- Using/eliminating temporary (Global/Volatile) tables

SOLUTION PLANNING

You can use the Teradata System Emulation Tool (SET) to test various changes before applying them to the production tables.

DBQL

You can use DBQL to log query processing activity to:

- Capture query/statement counts and response times.
- Discover potential application improvements.
- Make further refinements to workload groupings and scheduling.
- Have SQL text and processing steps analyzed.

DBQL provides a series of predefined tables that can store historical records of queries and their duration, performance, and target activity based on rules you specify. DBQL is flexible enough to log information on the variety of SQL requests, from short transactions to longer-running analysis and mining queries. You begin and end collection for a user or group of users and/or one or a list of accounts.

In addition to being able to capture the entire SQL statement, DBQL also provides key insights into other aspects of a query such as whether it was aborted or delayed by TDWM, the start and end time. DBQL operates asynchronously. As a result, the logging activity has a much lower impact on the overall response time of given transactions.

Note: Once you have utilized DBQL to find queries needing performance optimization, then start doing WHERE clause analysis, and Explains on the queries. From there, apply optimization strategies that could include advanced physical design options such as AJIs, and collecting statistics.

TABLE DESIGN CONSIDERATIONS FOR QUERY PERFORMANCE

NUSI

When using NUPIs, you can define a secondary index for a table to give the Optimizer another option for faster set selection. Although the Optimizer may still choose a full-table scan even if you define an SI, it generally chooses the SI if it is more useful for optimizing repetitive and standardized queries.

Note: Multiple ANDed NUSIs might qualify for NUSI Bit Mapping. Sparse NUSIs can also improve performance.

Utilize PPI/MLPPI tables for Partition and Full Table Scan Elimination

Utilizing PPI and MLPPI tables with queries that specify the partitioning columns, partition elimination will reduce what would otherwise be an all-AMP, full-table scan to an all-AMP scan of only the partitions required for the query. The extent of partition elimination depends on the partitioning expressions, the conditions specified in the query, and the ability of the Optimizer to recognize such opportunities.

Join Indexes

Join Indexes and each have a unique role in enhancing the performance of queries without applying denormalization techniques. Therefore, Join Indexes can be utilized to create persistent pre-join and summary tables. Join Indexes maintain the ability to support a wide range of decision support and ad hoc queries (i.e. Aggregate Join Indexes (AJI)).

Fallback

Though Fallback increases the number of I/Os for INSERT, UPDATE, and DELETE operations, it does not add additional I/Os to SELECT operations. Furthermore, SELECTs against Fallback tables will still go through even if there are AMPs down, as long as there are not two AMPs in the same cluster down.

Note: The cost, of course, is twice the disk space.

Permanent Journals

Permanent Journals (Before/After) provide a way of protecting non-Fallback tables against the loss of an AMP. The DUAL option protects the Journal similar to Fallback for tables.

Also, Permanent Journals are time-oriented, and can be used to return tables to an earlier consistent state (CHECKPOINT).

RI Constraints

Referential Integrity means that every Foreign Key (FK) value matches an existing Primary Key (PK) value.

RI constraints prevent inserting child rows that do not have a parent row. It prevents modifying an FK value to reference a non-existent parent. It prevents deleting a parent that still has children.

These checks add overhead for INSERT and DELETE operations, and UPDATEs to columns involved in RI definitions.

Note: Soft RI is recommended on Teradata. For more information, please see Chapter 9.

Teradata 14 Solutions Development

Compression

Basically, compression enables more rows to be stored per physical block, which results in less overall blocks to store the data. In turn, this means less work is required during a query operation. Disk I/O is further reduced because the compressed values are more likely to be memory resident and don't require disk access. Compression is great for full table scan operations, and any extra CPU utilization for these efforts is negligible in today's Teradata systems.

The best candidates for compression are fixed-width columns with a small number of frequently occurring values. Even though these column characteristics are for the very best candidates, you may choose to compress other columns just to save space. This is perfectly legitimate.

Here are some general rules and facts about compression:

- Only fixed width columns can be compressed at present.
- Up to 255 values can be compressed per column, including NULL values.
- You can't compress primary index columns.
- You can't compress volatile or derived table columns.
- You can't compress referencing foreign key columns.
- Nulls are automatically compressed when the COMPRESS clause is assigned.
- There is also an 8192 byte/character limit for the entire list of compressed items.

Dual system architecture

Dual system architecture, also known as Dual Active Solutions, is provided by Teradata Replication Solutions.

SOLUTION PLANNING

Teradata Replication Solutions allows users to capture changes made to a specific set of tables in one database and apply those changes to corresponding tables in another database in near real-time.

Teradata decides, for each DML request, whether to "ship" data or SQL. In the former, changes are made to data on the Source system and those changes are shipped over to the Targer system. In the latter, the SQL is shipped over from the Source system and then executed on the Target system. Any DDL requests are automatically shipped over to the Target system. Shipping the DML and DDL statements rather than the changed rows is more efficient.

Replication can serve several purposes in database information management:

- Replication can provide a backup of specified table data in the event of problems with your source database.
- If your site has Teradata Dual Active Solutions, and one system becomes unavailable, the remaining system can automatically take over database operations. The data on the systems will have been automatically synchronized via replication. There are various database replication tools and methodologies available for use with Teradata Dual Active Solutions. GoldenGate Replication Products is one such tool.
- When implemented between Teradata Database and databases from other vendors, you can migrate data from one system to the other, making data accessible across the different environments. This capability can support data acquisition, and Active Data Warehousing.

Teradata Replication Solutions are made up of Teradata Database and GoldenGate Replication products.

The following diagram shows the various ways Replication Solutions can be used.

Teradata 14 Solutions Development

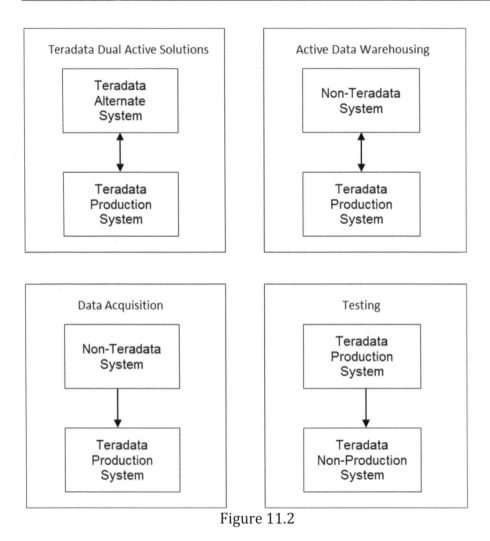

Figure 11.2

A dual active solution is a set of components or technologies that allow a secondary instance of Teradata Database to act as a backup for a primary instance of Teradata Database. Such a solution addresses a number of business continuity needs:

- Allows business operations to continue if a planned or unplanned outage occurs.
- Provides quick restoration of access to system resources.

SOLUTION PLANNING

- Enables businesses to enjoy consistent levels of service from their systems. Replication support is a key capability of a dual active solution. When implemented as part of Teradata Dual Active Solutions, Teradata Replication Solutions captures and synchronizes data between two instances of a database, where one is a production system and the other is a backup. As a result, the backup system can take over if the production system fails and maintain data availability and integrity.

The following diagram shows the architecture of a dual active system.

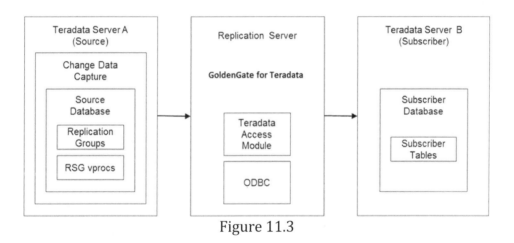

Figure 11.3

Teradata Replication Solutions can capture data from other types of databases and apply it to a Teradata Database. This data acquisition capability is not a replacement for a high-volume ETL (extract, transform, load) capability that requires significant transformation capabilities, but is designed to be used where:

- Real-time capture and apply is required
- There is a need to eliminate batch windows
- The volume of data that changes regularly is relatively moderate

- The customer wants to pull data from a non-Teradata database, minimizing the overhead to the source system

Note: Teradata Replication Solutions *does not* replace bulk data loading utilities, such as FastLoad and MultiLoad.

Chapter 11: Practice Questions

1. What kind of performance data should be collected?
    a. AMPUsage
    b. Data space
    c. DBQL data
    d. Heartbeat response times
    e. Resource usage data
    f. User counts
    g. All of the above

2. Columns appearing in a WHERE clause should have statistics collected on them _____.
    a. only if they are indexed
    b. only if they are not indexed
    c. whether they are indexed or not

3. Data compression _____ disk space and physical I/O.
    a. increases
    b. reduces

4. Which of the following can be compressed?.
    a. Variable width columns
    b. Fixed width columns
    c. Referencing foreign key columns
    d. PI columns
    e. Volatile table columns
    f. All of the above
    g. None of the above

5. When are Referential Integrity constraints enforced?
   a. Just on INSERTs
   b. Just on UPDATEs
   c. Just on DELETEs
   d. On any INSERT, UPDATE, or DELETE
   e. All of the above

6. Replication Solutions data acquisition _____ a replacement for bulk data loading utilities, such as FastLoad and MultiLoad.
   a. is
   b. is not

Chapter Notes

Utilize this space for notes, key points to remember, diagrams, areas of further study, etc.

APPENDIX A - Review Question Answers

Chapter 2	Chapter 3	Chapter 4
1. a 2. b 3. b 4. b 5. c	1. b 2. b 3. b 4. b 5. d 6. c 7. a 8. a, d 9. f 10. f 11. e	1. c 2. c 3. a 4. b 5. a 6. b, c, e 7. a 8. e 9. b
Chapter 5	**Chapter 6**	**Chapter 7**
1. a 2. b 3. c 4. c 5. a 6. c 7. a 8. a 9. a 10. b, e 11. c 12. d 13. a 14. e	1. c 2. c 3. d 4. a 5. b 6. b	1. b 2. b 3. c 4. a, c, d 5. c 6. c 7. a 8. c 9. b 10. c 11. b 12. b 13. b

Chapter 8	Chapter 9	Chapter 10
1. c 2. e 3. b 4. a 5. b 6. a	1. a, d 2. d 3. b 4. c, d 5. f 6. a, c, e, g 7. b, d, f, h 8. a 9. c 10. c	1. b 2. b 3. d 4. d 5. d 6. b 7. a 8. d 9. d 10. a 11. a 12. c 13. b 14. a
Chapter 11 1. g 2. c 3. b 4. b 5. d 6. b		

INDEX

A

Abort, 192
Access, 188, 199
ADO.NET, 238
AMP, 107, 158
AMP Worker Task, 203, 310
Analyst Pack, 293
AWT, 203, 310, 311, 312

B

BI, iv, 45, 231, 236
BLOBs, 177, 211
BTEQ, 56, 177, 178, 179, 180, 199, 200, 205, 211, 213, 214, 220, 221, 226, 241, 244, 262, 263, 271, 272
BYNET, ii

C

Call Level Interface, 238
Cartesian, 153
Certification, 1, 3, 6, 7, 8
Certified Professional, i, 1, 3, 8
CLI, 238
CLOBs, 177, 211
COMPRESS, 348
Compression, 348

D

Data, 238
Data Warehouse, 1
Date, 46, 65, 109, 111, 138, 141
DBC.AMPUsage, 326, 327
DBC.Columns, 304
DBC.Tables, 304
DBQL, 275, 277, 278, 281, 296, 298, 299, 345, 353

Disk I/O, 348

E

Exam, i, 1, 3, 5, 6, 7
Exclusion Join, 153
Explain, 151, 163, 164, 165, 170, 173, 280, 294, 295, 328, 329, 344

F

FastExport, 178, 185, 186, 187, 190, 194, 195, 199, 203, 204, 207, 210, 215, 218, 219, 222, 226, 235, 241, 245
FastLoad, 55, 105, 130, 140, 177, 181, 194, 195, 196, 199, 203, 204, 206, 210, 212, 213, 214, 218, 219, 220, 223, 224, 226, 227, 235, 241, 252, 256, 257, 271, 352, 354

G

GRANT, 306

H

Hash Join, 153

I

Index, 131, 132
Index Wizard, 293, 296, 297, 302
Indexes, 17, 19, 86, 91, 97, 102, 103, 104, 105, 127, 129, 130, 131, 132, 134, 138, 140, 142, 156, 276, 295, 344, 346

J

JDBC, 238
Join, 153

Join Index
   Multi-table, 134
Join Indexes, 346
Join Strategies, 153
Joins, 120, 121, 123, 129, 151, 152, 154, 156, 159, 160

L

Locking, 45, 46, 47, 50, 231, 242, 275, 324, 330
Locking Logger, 324, 325

M

Macros, 45, 56, 60, 61, 94, 174, 242, 264, 316
Merge Join, 153
MLPPI, 97, 110, 111, 112, 113, 114, 231, 244, 245, 346
MultiLoad, 55, 105, 130, 140, 177, 182, 188, 189, 190, 191, 192, 194, 195, 196, 199, 200, 203, 204, 207, 210, 215, 218, 219, 220, 223, 224, 226, 227, 235, 241, 244, 252, 256, 257, 271, 352, 354
Multi-Table Join Index, 134

N

Nested Join, 153
Nulls, 46, 75, 76, 77, 78, 79, 348
NUSI, 99, 100
NUSI Bit Mapping, 99, 100

O

ODBC, 238
OLAP, 10, 41, 64, 238
OLE DB, 238

P

performance, 107
Performance, 51, 152, 196, 231, 275, 279, 287, 288, 289, 290, 291, 292, 329, 343
Performance Groups, 287, 290
PI, 47, 91, 98, 103, 107, 133, 169, 222, 353
PMON, 275
PPI, 32, 35, 92, 93, 97, 106, 107, 109, 110, 113, 116, 120, 121, 122, 123, 124, 148, 171, 217, 231, 244, 245, 346
primary index, 107, 348
Primary Index, 158
Priority Scheduler, 284, 285, 288, 292, 293, 310, 311, 313
Product Join, 153
Product Joins, 160

R

RDBMS, 1
Resource Partitions, 287, 288, 289, 292
ResUsage, 224, 275, 309, 311, 314, 316, 320, 321, 322, 327, 330
Row Hash, 153
Row ID, 99

S

Schmon Utility, 293
SET/MULTISET, 26, 28, 39
SI, 98, 346
Statistics, 294, 295, 296, 298, 305, 306, 307, 311, 313
Statistics Wizard, 294, 295, 298
Summary Tables, 131

T

TASM, 275, 279
TDWM, 38, 284, 345
Technology, iv
Temporary Tables, 132

Teradata, i, ii, iv, 238
Teradata Administrator, ii
Time, 46, 65, 72, 73, 74, 291, 292
TPT, 105, 130, 177, 178, 195, 196, 197, 198, 199, 200, 203, 208, 211, 218, 220, 221, 222, 223, 224, 227, 241
TPump, 130, 177, 178, 192, 193, 194, 195, 200, 208, 216, 217, 218, 219, 222, 226, 227, 235, 241, 244, 245
Triggers, 231, 236, 249, 250, 251, 252
TSET, 280, 302, 303, 308

U

UDF, 249, 269, 270, 273
Unicode, 231, 243, 244
Upgrade, 3
Utilities, 4, 5, 143, 177, 252, 257

V

Views, 19, 45, 54, 55, 131, 234, 242, 314, 342
Visual Explain, 294, 298, 303